Expectations, Encouragement and Empowerment
- an Education:

An alternative to Targets, Testing and Tables
- a Tragedy

CYNTHIA BARTLETT

With thanks to the following for their support, advice and guidance:

The secondary headteachers of Oxfordshire – members of The Oxfordshire Secondary Schools Headteachers Association (OSSHTA)

Roger Dyson, Chair of Governors, Dr Jane Mellanby, Chair of the Governors' Curriculum and Assessment Committee, Jane Causon and Dave Hudson, Deputy Headteachers at Bicester Community College; Roy Blatchford, Director of the National Education Trust; Professor John Furlong, Director of the Department of Education, Oxford; The staff at Harris Manchester College, Oxford.

My gratitude also to Revd. Dr Ralph Waller, Principal, Harris Manchester College, Oxford who encouraged me and supported my secondment and to HSBC who funded the fellowship.

Cynthia Bartlett,
Headteacher, Bicester Community College, Oxfordshire.

Note: Quotations in italics at the beginning of each chapter are comments made by headteachers during interviews or within the questionnaire returns.

Published in the United Kingdom by Eirenikon Publishing
PO Box 591, Abingdon, Oxon, United Kingdom, OX14 9FW.

CONTENTS

Appendix 1   League Table to show order of
Oxfordshire schools 1993-2007

Appendix 2   Grid used in Inspection Reports to show
ECM compliance

Appendix 3a   Questionnaire sent to Oxfordshire
Headteachers (OSSHTA members)

Appendix 3b   Follow up questionnaire sent to
OSSHTA members December 2007.

"The true measure of a nation's standing is how well it attends to its children – their health and safety, their material security, their education and socialization, and their sense of being loved, valued, and included in the families and societies into which they are born."

Child Poverty in perspective: An overview of child well-being in rich countries. Report card 7 United Nation's Children's Fund 2007

INTRODUCTION

"The true measure of a nation's standing is how well it attends to its children – their health and safety, their material security, their education and socialization, and their sense of being loved, valued, and included in the families and societies into which they are born."

Child Poverty in perspective: An overview of child well-being in rich countries.
Report card 7 United Nation's Children's Fund 2007

The United Kingdom had for many years an enviable reputation for the quality of the education it provided for its children and for the methods of accreditation established for 16 and 18 year olds. There has been a tradition of pastoral care and a clear interest in the development of the whole person. In particular, schools have been seen not just to reflect the values of society but actively to promote values which were felt to be in the interests of a thoughtful, rational, peaceful society, content with itself and tolerant of others.

Education has always been subject to political pressure. However the pressures to which it has been subjected in the last twenty years or more, with an increasing tendency to micromanage, and an insistent demand for accountability, have led to adjustments in the public perception of the expectations of education. This study arose from an awareness that schools were coping with increasing numbers of vulnerable young people, and a recognition of two powerful trends in educational policy and practice. The first of these is a need on the part of governments to gain credit and prove success, leading to an increased emphasis on 'standards'- largely academic standards. There has followed the introduction of the National Curriculum and increased assessment by national testing of a small part of the school curriculum at fixed points. This in turn

1

has resulted in the present target culture and in league tables. The second trend has been a discernable movement towards a utilitarian approach in which education is only as good as the preparation it provides for employment. This has led to the culture of value being attached only to that which may be measured, education strategies and policies following business and market models and a rejection or marginalisation of curriculum not seen to be 'useful'.

Despite the rhetoric on the centrality of the child and more recently on student voice, the focus in education has moved away from the children themselves, to their treatment as the means to ends. In the midst of these developments, those who are in danger of greatest harm and need the most attention are vulnerable young people for whom education may become merely an unwanted distraction within their daily lives. In a life which now may encompass eighty years or more, eleven are spent in compulsory education and it is important to reflect on fundamental questions about what is expected of these early formative years. When personality and interests are developing and talents and skills are being acquired, what does society need to achieve? What does it require of a young person in their twenties beginning to make a major contribution to the society in which they live and work? What should society expect education to provide for young people? What human qualities should education be encouraging? How can education empower young people as citizens? A UNICEF report (2007) concludes:

> "Many therefore feel that it is time to attempt to re-gain a degree of understanding, control and direction over what is happening to our children in their most vital, vulnerable years."[1]

The 1944 Education Act set out the purposes of education for all:

---

[1] UNICEF (2007) An overview of child well-being in rich countries. Report Card 7 p39

"It shall be the duty of the LEA for every area, so far as their powers extend, to contribute towards the spiritual, moral, mental and physical development of the community by securing that efficient education throughout those stages shall be available to meet the needs of the population of this area."[2]

There is here a broad definition of the difference which education should make to a community, and the recognition that the needs of each area should be taken into account. In 1977 the Department for Education and Science in Education for Schools (DES and Welsh office) set out once more the aims of education and these were repeated in 'Better Schools' (1985) They have been widely adopted by local authorities and individual schools:

- To help pupils develop lively, enquiring minds, the ability to question and argue rationally and to apply themselves to tasks, and physical skills
- To help pupils to acquire understanding, knowledge and skills relevant to adult life and employment in a fast-changing world
- To help pupils to use language and number effectively
- To help pupils to develop personal moral values, respect for religion and tolerance of other races, religions and ways of life.
- To help pupils to understand the world in which they live, and the interdependence of individuals, groups and nations
- To help pupils to appreciate human achievements and aspirations

Such aims have continued to be expressed in Education Acts in recent times. The Education Act 2002 required all maintained schools to provide a balanced and broadly based curriculum that:

- promotes the spiritual, moral, cultural, mental and physical development of learners at the school and within society.

---

[2] Stages and Purposes of Statutory System Education. 1944 Education Act

- prepares learners at the school for the opportunities, responsibilities and experiences of adult life.[3]

Few would disagree with such aims. Yet those working in education are frequently questioning the direction which education is taking. Of concern are the results of the UNICEF survey of 21 OECD countries (2007) in which the UK appears at the bottom of the table on Child Well-Being. The Convention on the Rights of the Child indicates that children's circumstances should allow 'the development of the child's personality, talents and mental and physical abilities to their fullest potential'. This is measured in six dimensions – material well-being, health and safety, educational well-being, family and peer relationships, behaviour and risks and subjective well-being. In the latter three the UK is ranked last.

One of the causes of some of the greatest difficulties schools have faced in recent years has been a decision to place education within a 'market' driven system. Governments and politicians have seen parents, not pupils, as the consumers of education and have increasingly expected institutions to be run on a business model. (Whitty et al. 1998; Merrett 2006) The 'market' model has led to increased accountability and bureaucracy, treating schools as businesses and regarding students as products, the quality of which can be numerically assessed. Thus gains or achievements which are immeasurable are seen as unimportant or irrelevant. Teachers have become 'deliverers' of a given body of knowledge which, according to government agencies, if only they were to deliver it in the correct way, would lead to massively improved product outcomes i.e. improved test and examination results. The Government meanwhile acts as a Board of Directors and expects to produce more and better quality products each year. If its workers do not conform and 'deliver the goods', severe penalties are imposed and increased pressure brought to bear. There are also

---

[3] The National Curriculum: statutory requirements for key stages 3 and 4 2007 DCSF & QCA

incentives such as performance related pay or special rewards for which 'good' schools may have the privilege of bidding. Meanwhile, despite the stated emphasis on 'student voice', the 'product' has little say in the matter. If its English, maths and science attainment are at least at the 'expected' level when tested at regular intervals, then it is satisfactory. If not, it has failed and is rejected - and in a blame culture, the 'Board of Directors' seeks to punish those responsible – schools, teachers, parents. (This is of course a caricature of a well-run business which understands more about ownership and team work and does not subscribe to this particular market model.)

In this competitive climate, collaboration is often seen, not as a productive partnership of schools in which good practice can be shared and all contribute and receive equally, but as a tool for levering up standards in poor schools by association with better schools. If this is unsuccessful, then schools will be closed. The students, meanwhile, are pawns in the game in which many vulnerable young people will not even take part.

> "The increasingly competitive nature of education which requires further control of the disaffected, the disadvantaged and those with 'special needs' who may not contribute to the economy, is not socially just." (Thrupp and Tomlinson, 2005)

This study has consisted of a survey of research conducted in these areas largely after 1992, when league tables were first introduced. It has also included the views of secondary headteachers in Oxfordshire obtained through questionnaires, informal conversations and individual interviews. Of 34 secondary schools in Oxfordshire, five had newly appointed headteachers in the year of the research and did not comment. Of the remaining 29 headteachers, 20 returned questionnaires and two others sent written responses. Of these 8 were interviewed together with the Headteacher of the Meadowbrook College (Pupil Referral Unit provision) The headteachers interviewed were chosen to represent

5

different kinds of secondary schools - 11-16 and 11-18, rural and urban, their schools placed in different positions in the league table for 5 A*-C. Their views include reflections on the influence on national policy on practice in their schools and on the extent to which they have interpreted government policies in ways which would enable basic principles to be pursued, integrity to be sustained and vision to be upheld. They are aware of the dilemmas set for them by policies which are often contradictory. They know that local authorities are under pressure to comply with government demands and recognise that a positive relationship with their Local Authority is at times difficult to sustain as it enforces policies which prioritise testing, targets and readiness for inspection and appears to judge achievement merely on test and examination results. They understand the issues for young people and their families as their schools seek to serve them and they recognise the particular concerns which relate to vulnerable students and their inclusion.

In this study of the effect of targets, testing and league tables, I have used the word 'vulnerable' to describe the young people concerned. Vulnerability may be observed in the behaviour of individuals in terms of truancy, school refusal, criminality, addiction, anti-social behaviour at home or in school or in the attitudes of some young people towards their education – disaffected, under-achieving, alienated, unhappy. Anxiety suffered by students across the ability range creates another kind of vulnerability. Vulnerable students are often those who have social as well as educational problems, and disaffection, truancy, disruption and exclusion are disproportionately found in disadvantaged groups (Parsons 1999). Very few permanently excluded students are of above average ability (Ofsted 1996) and nearly half of these students have literacy difficulties. Ofsted has reported that there are now 200,000 young people not in education, employment or training (NEET). Yet education, given appropriate support and funding, can open doors, alleviate some of the effects of social disadvantage and prevent deprivation from one generation to another. This study looks at some current barriers to such success which are rooted in present government policies. At the same time, it considers what education can and should provide for all, with particular reference to these groups, as it contributes to the happiness, peace and well-being of a society.

It is my intention to minimise the word 'improve' in this study. The phrase 'school improvement' has become a mantra in the last decade and this in itself has had an undermining effect on public confidence. If a director announces publicly that his firm will produce 'an improved service', the public know and understand that he is answering criticism of a service – otherwise he would be speaking of 'development' or 'enhancement'. The DSCF, politicians, local councillors and some educationalists have continued relentlessly to refer to 'school improvement'. This alone gives the public cause for alarm. Consideration needs to be given to the vocabulary used to develop school effectiveness and to recognise school achievement. When, to this use of critical vocabulary, is added direct attacks on state education, on individual schools and on standards in assessment, public confidence is undermined, confusion and uncertainty increase and many students and their parents may begin to believe that their state education is second-rate and valueless.

The 'Every Child Matters' policy document (2003)[4], recommends five outcomes for children and young people which affirm positive values and a commitment to all. In autumn 2007, the Prime Minister urged parents to play a bigger part in school life with 'more parents' sessions' at school to share information and set goals[5]. No one would doubt that parents' involvement in the education of their children is crucial and enhances their chances of success, but the messages are confusing, especially to parents of vulnerable young people. On one hand, Home-School agreements

---

[4] Every Child Matters (2003) Green Paper Published by The Stationery Office
[5] A Blair, speech at Greenwich University London 31st October 2007

emphasise a positive partnership between school staff and parents in the establishment of a confident relationship of trust. On the other hand, fines, parenting orders and governors' discipline committees apportion blame, create stress and alienate. Meanwhile, policies indicate that in fact some children matter more than others and thus many young people continue to miss opportunities which would lead to a lifetime of positive experiences in learning.

A more hopeful development in the emphasis on the care, nurture and education of young people has been The Children Act 2004 and the bringing together of services for Children, Young People and Families. In the light of the Victoria Climbié Report and reports following other well publicised tragedies, it is important that the needs of all members of a family are considered, that communication between agencies is good and that work with a family is well planned and coordinated. Staff in schools have for many years recognised their responsibilities 'in loco parentis'. The status has perhaps too long been disregarded by many, resulting in an underestimation of the time and energy school staff give daily to the support of young people and their parents – often in relation to circumstances well outside the school's official remit. If schools are responsible for young people for seven or eight hours a day, it is to be expected that staff will act as careful parents during this time. For some vulnerable young people, the building up of these relationships of trust and of the three-way partnership between themselves, their parents and the school staff is important and may have a significant effect on lives. For others, staff act as surrogate parents and students' encounter with kindness, concern and encouragement may be an experience restricted to school hours.

This study, in focusing on vulnerable students, recognises the parenting role which schools undertake. As the study progressed, it was clear that the effects of targets, testing and league tables on the teaching profession and all those who support young people in school could not be ignored. The impact of policy on the adults in the system had repercussions on young people in the schools and especially perhaps on the vulnerable. A recent study on the effects of inspection, increasingly a part of the system of accountability and performance-driven policies, asserts that "The sense of being permanently under a disciplinary regime can lead to fear, anger and disaffection" (Perryman, 2007 p173) Such emotions might not seem conducive to the retention of a well-motivated, highly qualified workforce which sees its work as rewarding as well as challenging. The question has to be asked, 'Are such policies encouraging and empowering the workforce to make good the deficit with which many young people enter education, or is the deficit gap widening during the years of compulsory education?'

The study has investigated the extent to which government policy is supporting schools as the surrogate parents, in the education of vulnerable young people. The hypothesis is that current policies do not promote learning and impede the capacity to meet demands and serve communities. Learning takes place when motivation is good and when praise follows performance. It is enhanced by high expectations and careful encouragement. It leads to empowerment not only of individuals, but of groups and communities. If education promotes the realisation of potential, then the same positive strategies known to be successful with learners, and particularly vulnerable learners, need to be consistently applied to schools.

The education of vulnerable young people is affected by the ethos of the schools they attend and the capacity of those schools to meet their needs. Do current policies enhance the capacity of schools to develop young people as well-educated parents and citizens of the future, or do they provide additional barriers to a positive experience of learning? Are the values promoted heavily by central policy the values which society as a whole wants to promote?

The study does not attempt to examine the causes or possible cures for the social problems and challenges facing young people.

However, it may present some insight into what school leaders believe their schools are currently contributing in order to raise achievement and encourage learning and how they and their schools work to alleviate some of the effects of poverty, poor parenting, low self-esteem and alienation. It may also provide opportunities to reflect on what more might be done to close the achievement gap, reduce the NEET (Not in Education, Employment or Training) numbers and contribute to the happiness and well-being of local communities and their families from one generation to the next.

EXPECTATIONS

HAPPINESS

"We want them to be well-adjusted, confident people, who understand happiness and recognise justice"

"We aim to create a safe, caring but challenging environment where all students have a sense of belonging, enjoy learning and are able to thrive."

The most important desire of a parent for their child is that they should be happy. Happiness is paramount – it is what a well-functioning family wants for itself and for its individual members. It comes before success or wealth or public recognition; all these may contribute to happiness, but most know that they are not essential. What people say they want most for themselves and for others is happiness, well-being and peace.

A yearly summary of averages from the Schools Survey produced by Keele University (2004)[6], based on the responses of over 50,000 students, reported that 88% of pupils are usually happy at school and 88% of parents are happy with their children's schools. This supports an earlier survey on attitudes to school, in which the majority of students, approximately 90%, slightly more girls than boys, held positive attitudes to school (Keys et al. 1995)[7]. This is an important and perhaps not unexpected finding despite the unwelcome adverse publicity which state schools have been receiving. Parents place great store on their children's happiness. They want their children to do well and gain qualifications, but they do not judge schools on examination results alone. They

---

[6] Year averages (2004) Schools Survey – Keele University, Centre for Successful Schools reported in Times Educational Supplement W Mansell 9.11.07
[7] Keys Wendy, Fernandes 1995 What students think about School. *A report for the National Commission on Education* Slough NFER.

search for more information than academic results alone because of greater importance to them are issues of happiness and welfare. They value personal recommendation and local knowledge. The Headmasters and Headmistresses Conference, has published a guide for parents in which it explains what league tables will and will not show and provides parents with guidance on other information they should seek. It confirms:

> "**Most importantly of all** [bold in document] league tables do not tell you whether your child will be happy and will thrive"[8]

Teachers know that children who are unhappy will not learn. They may be unhappy because they are neglected at home, or because they have few or no friends. They may be unhappy because they have low self-esteem and view themselves as failures. They may be unhappy because demands on them, at home or at school, are too high, too low, inappropriate or inconsistent. Whatever the reasons, children who are unhappy are unlikely to make good progress; they are busy surviving, their agenda is elsewhere. Thus, those variously described as disadvantaged, disaffected, vulnerable or challenging arrive in school with barriers to learning which the school must address if learning is to be a positive experience.

One recent survey stated that one in ten children move to secondary school with no friends after huge competition to get into the 'best' comprehensives.[9] This trend has been more noticeable recently with the advent of the league tables and has exacerbated the problem of falling rolls in some schools and oversubscription in others. A quarter of 11 year olds are found to leave at least one of their best friends behind, leading to anxiety.[10] Most students, after an initial period of anxiety, adjust quickly to a new school and make new friends, but some find this aspect of the change

---

[8] HMC School League Tables (2004) What they tell you…and what they don't. *Advice to Parents and Other Interested Parties Information* Page 5
[9] Report Daily Telegraph 2007 1st November
[10] Daily Telegraph 1st November 2007 Page 10

traumatic and find new relationships much more difficult to establish. They become unhappy and lose self-confidence; they become vulnerable. Friendships are important and relationships with other students figure greatly in the research on disaffection. (Riley and Rustique Forrester, 2002; Riley and Docking, 2004)

Learning to make and keep relationships, to deal with intolerance and to develop confidence in socialising is a key element in the security and happiness of any individual. Great unhappiness can arise from bullying and young people who are or believe they are being bullied are unhappy and vulnerable. They cannot learn. Schools spend much time and effort addressing such issues. Incidents happen in the community as well as in school; sometimes whole families are engaged in feuds, and police may be involved. With the advent of MSN[11], texting and webcams, bullying takes on a new menace, becoming an ever-present threat, even in the 'safety' of home. In a study of the views of truants, students expressed views that bullying was ignored by their school, indicating that teachers did not have the time to be interested in sorting out difficulties (Hilton 2006). While inspection reports indicate that many schools deal well with bullying, the fact that schools are employing more support staff, who do not have teaching commitments, indicate the need for intervention by the school in many social situations such as these. Such staff, together with tutors, and year leaders are dealing with fundamental issues which make young people unhappy and impede their learning.

One form of bullying which exists in schools, often in subtle forms difficult to address, is academic bullying. Reay and Wiliam (1999) noted in their study[12] of one Year 6 class that as the KS2 SATs approached, the child who had previously been identified by the children as the brightest in the class, began to get isolated and

---

[11] Microsoft Network or Multiple Subscriber Number
[12] Reay Diane, Wiliam Dylan (1999)'I'll be a nothing': structure, agency and the construction of identity through assessment.' *British Educational Research Journal* 25 (3) pp343-354

bullied as practice tests revealed he was ahead of his peers. The children explained their change in behaviour by indicating that he was now showing off, but the researcher present in the classroom knew this was in fact not the case. As more and more practice test results were declared, anxiety rose within the class, and bullying commenced. Similar situations can arise in secondary schools, often related to peer pressure, and students become isolated; some give up work and others work chiefly in the privacy of their homes, deciding that maintaining relationships is a greater priority at school.

While many students face considerable barriers to learning from factors outside the school, it is clear that vulnerable students may feel isolated or alienated in different ways from much that they perceive the school stands for - its structure, its rules and its culture. Writing just before league tables appeared, Furlong (1991)[13] reports on the 'complex pattern of injuries' that school can produce and urges professionals to consider, alongside individual needs and traumas, ways in which the culture of an institution may contribute to or increase students' emotional injuries.

Young people will take steps to protect themselves. If academic doors are shutting and the prevalent culture alienates them, they may create a sub-culture which provides different goals, values and behaviours. Furlong (1991) suggests once young people have a supportive sub-culture, and "a rationale for rejecting school, then they are much more difficult to bring back into line"[14] It may be that the present emphasis on the top end of academic achievement promotes the creation of subcultures, as low reading age, English as a second language, common dysfunctional backgrounds and

---

[13] VJ Furlong *Disaffected Pupils: Reconstructing the Sociological Perspective* British Journal of Sociology of Education Vol 12 No 3 (1991) p293-307
[14] VJ Furlong Disaffected Pupils: Reconstructing the Sociological Perspective. *British Journal of Sociology of Education* 12 No 3 (1991) p293-307

other factors lead to slow progress and perceived failure (Kinder, 1997; Lovey, 1999).

Headteachers interviewed in the study were clear about their role in leading a happy school community in which all students could flourish. They recognised the need to provide more support staff to deal with pastoral matters, to provide nurture for individuals and the small group work which would have a positive impact on vulnerable students. The majority of the schools were providing breakfast, open to all students (68%) and of the remainder, 17% were assisting specifically vulnerable students who routinely arrived at school having had nothing to eat or drink. They were aware that many of their staff were engaged in parenting roles and knew that such activity contributed to the happiness and success which individual students would experience. Riley and Docking (2004) support this view: "heads and teachers can make a difference to the way students feel about school, even among schools in the most disadvantaged areas."[15]

Headteachers were equally convinced of the need to promote a culture in which their staff would develop and thrive. Teaching is a profession of service to the community. Happiness at work comes largely from knowing that individual children have been well served and that individual teachers have played a part in ensuring that students have achieved their potential. The fact that the vast majority of students report that they are happy at school and that many staff find their work rewarding, despite the demands, is testimony to the values on which schools have stood firm in the face of much pressure to concentrate only on what can be measured. Stability for young people outside the home often rests on the stability of the school community. Students are perceptive, are aware of the ways in which teachers' feelings of satisfaction, optimism and goodwill pervade their classrooms and affect

---

[15] Riley Kathryn, Docking Jim Voices of Disaffected pupils: Implications for Policy and Practice. *British Journal of Educational Studies* 52 No 2 June 2004 pp166-179

teaching and learning. Headteachers are aware that, if the ethos of their schools is to highlight positive values staff, as well as students, need to feel fulfilled and properly rewarded.

Cohort results will vary from year to year but a community school cannot afford to lurch from praise to castigation from one year to the next. Reputations are hard won, but easily destroyed. Currently schools can move speedily in the Local Authority's view from 'effective' to 'a school of concern', from Ofsted's 'good' category to special measures, largely on the basis of GCSE results. This confuses and upsets communities – it demoralises staff and unsettles students (Searle, 2001; Parsons, 2005). Research indicates that where teachers are seen to be anxious, fearful of poor academic results and concerned about their jobs, students catch the insecurity and the unhappiness and are affected by it. (Reay and Wiliam, 1999; Perryman, 2007)

There has been support for young people receiving lessons in well-being and happiness (SEAL - the social and emotional aspects of learning) and a public school headteacher recently introduced lessons in 'happiness' into the curriculum.[16] Such programmes certainly underline the basic needs of young people. However, as with so many other kinds of learning, first-hand experience is by far the best way to learn. If young people and schools as a whole were not put into unnecessary and artificially-created situations of stress and anxiety, they would be sure to increase their experience of happiness and well-being. Staff in schools know that taking part in sports teams, school productions, extra-curricular activities, residentials, public speaking, art clubs etc. provides children with much satisfaction and happiness. If academic work is to provide for more of this kind of contentment and pleasure, changes need to be made. If schools are able to concentrate fully on a broad and balanced curriculum with sufficient personalisation of learning and

---

[16] Anthony Seldon, Headmaster of Wellington School. Teaching happiness is no laughing matter 25.5.2007 Telegraph.co.uk

funding to ensure appropriate pace and challenge, then most young people will at least understand what it is to be happy, even if their lives impact on their ability to make uniform academic progress through a specific period of time. Vulnerable young people need much reassurance about the potential to be happy about their work and the opportunity to see their school as a safe, peaceful haven in which they can grow.

Peter Wilby, a former editor of the 'New Statesman' in responding to the announcement of the SEAL[17] initiative suggests that lifting people out of poverty is a much more effective step to happiness. He comments, "schools can teach useful, interesting and stimulating things. Music, poetry, sport, drama dance, science, nature, architecture, cooking, even maths – all can touch the human soul and if some children are too emotionally damaged to appreciate them, therapists may be able to help, but not I think teachers."[18] This is an important point. There is no doubt of the demands for increased availability of mental health expertise. Schools are attempting to reach students whose needs in this area are great; but expert help is often difficult to harness, delayed in arriving and short in duration.

It may be seen therefore that creating an ethos of happiness is a top priority for schools. The ingredients of happiness - stability, security, good health, positive relationships, self-confidence - lead to motivation, creativity, achievement, success and a life-long desire for learning. Indeed research has indicated that if students have poor experiences at school, their view of education does not change as they get older. Of course, a child who has a 'happy' home has a head start, but all will benefit from a happy school, a second home, and the most vulnerable will stand to gain the most.

---

[17] Social and Emotional Aspects of Learning'
[18] Wilby Peter 'Well-being? Ending poverty comes first'. *Times Educational Supplement* 29th September 2007

ACHIEVEMENT

"The targets per se do not have this effect (i.e. raising standards); it is our self-generated desire to achieve the best that we can for the students that has driven school improvement"

"We have always focused on students achieving on the vocational courses at whatever level (despite the impact this increasingly seems to have on our average points score or value added figures.)"

"Insistence on the 5A*-C is a tragedy. It reinforces failure. Students not likely to achieve this are aware of this very early – it is rammed down their throats."

While headteachers recognised that the achievements for students in their schools were many and varied, achievement nationally now appears to equate with performance in national examinations and the performance of individuals in relation to their prior attainment or in value-added scores. The effect on schools of these measures, together with the current emphasis on target setting and league tables, has been considerable. In order to study their specific effect on vulnerable young people, it is necessary to have an understanding of the demands and pressures placed on schools, on their time, their curriculum strategies and their budgets by such policies and by the current 'standards' agenda.

There appears to be a reluctance on the part of some educationalists, possibly as a result of the inappropriate market comparisons, to acknowledge that students' academic abilities differ. There also appears to be confusion between criteria and norm-referenced testing. By the very nature of the kinds of academic testing undertaken, students are not able to recall or understand the content or to cope equally with the demands of any given specification. Examination Boards, while ensuring that papers are accessible to all, seek to differentiate across a wide range of candidates and to achieve a healthy standard deviation. If the population, on a cognitive abilities test, for example, can be said to be plotted on a normal distribution, then approximately half will be 'below average'. Yet it appears a small step to move from an average level or grade to an 'expected' level, allowing those below the average to be 'failing'[19]

Given a stable intake, and good teacher understanding of examination requirements, if specifications and other variables remained the same, one would expect the 5 A*-C result (with English and maths) to stabilise. If it continued to rise year on year, it would be reasonable to draw the conclusion that either the examination grade boundaries have been lowered, the specifications have been reduced in demand or, in the case of an individual school, that the school is no longer fully comprehensive. It is possible that with the inclusion of other kinds of assessment, in vocational courses for example, GCSE equivalence will enable a rise in the percentage of 5 A*-C grades. However, given the absence of any further variables, and the current emphasis on maths, it is difficult to see how or why percentages rates of those achieving at least 5 A*-C including GCSE English and maths at 16 could be expected to rise relentlessly year on year.

It would appear that 5 A*-C grades are now regarded as a measure of success to which all students should aspire. However, GCSE was designed for 85% of students in schools (not 100%) and was to award pass grades at different levels. A*-C grades were roughly equivalent to the old O-Level grades and D-G to the CSE grades. The move to a national examination at 16 was designed to give all students equal opportunities and at first D-G grades were not spoken of as 'fail' grades. In recent years however, the benefits to

---

[19] Daily Telegraph 28 February 2008 'One in three pupils fails to reach target in core subjects'

students, who previously would have taken CSEs and now take GCSEs, have been taken away. Their reward for achievement, a grade at GCSE, is removed and a D categorised as a 'fail'. Thus attempts to improve performance and provide equal opportunities for all through comprehensive education and one common examination have come to grief and those who lose the most are those whom society can least afford to reject.

> "The measure of five good passes perpetuates the historic divisions in English education between O-Level sheep and CSE goats, between educating learners and training followers (c.f Edwards 1997); it also intensifies the polarization of performance between highly successful and poorly achieving schools with 56 per cent of 16 year olds gaining five good GCSEs, which means 44 per cent still do not." [20]

It is widely recognised (Thrupp, 1999; Miliband, 2004) that "academic attainment tends to be low in schools with high proportions of pupils of low income homes" and is generally low in schools serving poor neighbourhoods. Lack of well-informed parental support, financial backing and benign peer pressure contribute to low attainment, as do racial inequality, family disruption, low educational ambition and weaknesses in useful academic skills, in literacy and independent learning (Bell, 2003). Headteachers supported this view, including family dysfunction and attendance difficulties and low aspirations as reasons for underachievement in public examinations.

Tymms (2004) has questioned the validity of the statutory tests in primary schools, and recommends that "statutory test data must not be used to monitor standards over time." Different tests are set each year which restricts their use in monitoring standards. He notes that the early rise in standards (1995-2000) was likely to be

---

[20] Coffield Frank 2006 "Running Ever Faster Down the Wrong Road: An Alternative Future for Education and Skills." Inaugural Lecture 5th December 2006.

partly the result of teaching test technique and teaching to the test. He called for an independent body to be established with the sole purpose of monitoring standards over time.[21] Earl et al. (2003) reported "doubts about whether increases in test scores actually represents comparable increases in pupil learning"[22]. Alan Smithers, commenting on examination statistics said: "Better examination scores are only good news if they stand for corresponding increases in underlying understanding."[23] Another study of the effects of testing concluded, "The more specific the Government is about what it is that schools are to achieve, the more likely it is to get it, but the less likely it is to mean anything."[24] (Reay and Wiliam 1999)

There is some evidence that perceptions of the success and impact of target-setting differs depending on the year by year results of the school concerned. Davies et al. (2005)[25] noted that teachers in schools with a higher than 50% 5A*-C were more likely to own the target-setting process and believe it was effective in raising standards. Schools performing at lower than 50% 5A*-C, were experiencing difficulties that made the target setting process harder to implement. It was then more difficult to own the process, targets could be seen as unrealistic and the incentive factor for teachers was diminished. Davies et al. (2005) also indicates that teachers

---

[21] Tymms Peter 2004 Are standards rising in English primary schools? *British Educational Research Journal* 30 No 4 2004 pp 477-494

[22] Earl L.M., Fullan, M., Leithwood, K & Watson, N. (2000) Watching and Learning 3: OISE/UT evaluation of the Implementation of the Literacy and Numeracy Strategies. Nottingham, DfEE Publications P 12

[23] Smithers Alan, Education and Employment Research Centre , University of Buckingham The Times August 29th 2007

[24] Reay Diane Wiliam Dylan (1999) I'll be a nothing: structure, agency and the constriction of identity through assessment. *British Educational Research Journal* 25 (3) Pp343-354   P 353

[25] Davies, Peter, Coates Gwen, Hammersley-Fletcher, Linda and Mangan, Jean. (2005) When becoming a 50% school is success enough: a principal-agent analysis of subject leaders' target setting. *School Leadership and Management* 25:5 493-511

when saying 'Our pupils simply cannot achieve this' may not necessarily have low expectations – they may just be aware of a reduced capability, given increasing levels of need, poor behaviour, lack of motivation and support from home. The study emphasises the need for self-direction by teachers. The more they believe that policies are externally imposed, the less they will own them or seek to implement them.

The responses of headteachers broadly supported these views. They expected to set targets based on data for the specific cohort, which would not result necessarily in a higher target than the previous year, in consultation with their staff, their School Improvement Partner and their governors. They did not expect the Local Authority to intervene in this procedure, and in most cases it did not. This may be due to the adoption by a number of the schools in Oxfordshire of the Fischer Family Trust (FFT) D[26] whole school estimate or of a target which lay between FFTD and B[27], with which the LA would be unlikely to disagree. In schools which had lower 5A*-C percentages, where the LA would be concerned about 'under-achievement' and did attempt to influence target-setting, headteachers endeavoured to hold a line on realistic expectations, knowing that staff morale and motivation, and community confidence would not be improved by the setting of targets which were unlikely to be met. This approach would appear to be one supported by Fischer Family Trust itself which emphasises that FFTD figures are estimates and not targets. In a paper on the role of Local Authorities in supporting School Improvement, Durrant (2007) argues that 'sustaining' standards might be a sensible approach, since forever raising standards leads to "a treadmill from which nobody can ever escape"[28]

---

[26] The set of figures which equate to "similar to the progress made by pupils in the 'top 24%' of schools nationally last year".

[27] The set of figures which equate to "the same as the progress made by pupils in similar schools".

[28] Durrant Danny (2007) The role of UK Local Authorities to support school improvement. Paper presented at the British Educational Research Association

However, schools are encouraged to plan and operate strategies for ever greater student achievement in tests and examinations and the majority of Oxfordshire schools involved in the study were doing so. Much sway was held by booster classes and catch-up sessions and certainly they have been seen to make a difference to test results (Bell 2003)[29]. Yet there is concern that these short-term gains do not focus on the real long term issues facing schools with many disadvantaged students. Boyle et al. (2006) reports that nationally a *minority* of schools seem to have take up such strategies and many are still seen to be under-achieving. He asks why such schools are not taking the most obvious remedial action. It may be that schools have decided that there are more pressing issues and priorities which they need to address. Boyle asks "Is the range of 'real' social and cultural problems so great that national test outcomes, league table performance and its attendant 'status' not a priority." He suggests that the current standards agenda may simply not be seen to be relevant to 'an increasing percentage of the nation's schools.' Davies et al. (2005) also points out that the differences between approaches to targets taken by different schools may reflect "sensible responses of schools with higher proportions of pupils with lower absolute attainments" and that they may be making choices about focusing on outcomes such as social skills "because the potential gain is greater"[30]. A government evaluation report on the implementation of literacy and numeracy strategies, which is fairly inconclusive, makes the point that "setting even higher national targets may no longer serve to mobilise and motivate, particularly if schools see the targets as unrealistic" (Earl et al. 2003)[31]

Annual Conference, Institute of Education, University of London, 5-7 September 2007

[29] Bell D (2003) Access and achievement in urban education; 10 years on. A speech to the Fabian Society, London

[30] Davies John Dwyfor and Lee John Part 2 barriers to responsiveness in three disadvantaged schools. page 510

[31] Earl L.M., Fullan, M., Leithwood, K & Watson, N. (2003) Watching and Learning 3: OISE/UT evaluation of the Implementation of the Literacy and Numeracy Strategies Nottingham, DfEE Publications page 7

Gorard (2005) notes that raw-score performance figures were heavily dependent on prior attainment and family background of students. Given this 'fundamental flaw', Wales decided to withdraw the publication of school results in 2001. Gorard then looked at the value-added figures for 2004 and concluded that there were unexpectedly high correlations between indicators of overall school attainment and the value-added figures from each key stage. The highest (+0.96) was between the KS4 absolute score for each school and the value-added scores for progress between KS3 and KS4. He concludes "In fact we could predict the value-added figure for any school extremely well just from their absolute level of final attainment."[32] In the study there were no low to mid-attaining schools with high value-added scores. All of the schools with a GCSE benchmark of 40% or less were deemed negative value-added. At the time of the study, contextual value-added was proposed. Gorard comments "This may mask, but will not solve the problem described here."[33] Jesson (2007) urges caution as he notes the common misuses of Contextual Value Added (CVA) measures. He emphasises that schools cannot be ranked by one CVA measure alone and the upper and lower confidence limits need to be taken into account. He warns:

> "'We have many reports of inspections where this simple provision has been ignored. CVA values are 'ranked' and schools are then told that they are underperforming if their CVA measure is below 1000. This must cease."[34]

A number of research projects have questioned the ability of secondary schools to change radically their 'effectiveness' as judged by raw results or even with a value-added perspective. One study (Thomas, Peng and Gray 2007) looked at cohorts of students

---

[32] Gorard Stephen (2005) Value-added is of little value. Paper presented at Br Educational Research Association Annual Conference Glamorgan
[33] Ibid.
[34] Jesson David (2007)The use and misuse of CVA. *British Educational Research Association in Research Intelligence* 100 p 23

over a decade, thus studying a period of 15 years from when the first students began their secondary school career to the time the tenth cohort left. It concluded that in terms of raw data, none of the schools that started out in 1993 performing significantly lower than expected had transformed themselves into institutions performing 'significantly higher' by 2002. Moreover 92% of schools in the 'significantly higher' category in 1993 were still in the same category ten years later. Even when value added considerations were taken into account, and taking 'improvement' to be any upward movement, just 17% of schools were able to improve for at least four years in succession at some point during the decade. Three years of upward movement seemed to be the typical limit. These findings would not support government demands for 'continuous school improvement' if measured in this way.

> "For the vast majority of schools, 'transformation' of their relative position, status and reputation remains an elusive prospect even when they are apparently successful in achieving some degree of improvement over time."[35]

This study also indicated that the publication of league tables had not substantially changed schools' relative positions over time although value added had resulted in a more fluid situation. The position of the Oxfordshire schools over the last 15 years (Appendix 1) supports the research here. It is also clear that value-added scores based on prior attainment will only be as good as the quality of the previous test. The English KS3 test for example has proved notoriously unreliable. The new requirement for two levels of progress is unlikely to improve the situation. It is difficult to see how it can be in the interests of students that, in relation to this new measure, schools will have to hope that students do not over-achieve at one level of national tests. If they do, the school may not be able to show an increase of two levels of progress at the next

---

[35] Thomas Sally, Peng Wen Jung, and Gray, John (2007) Value added trends in English secondary education school performance across ten cohorts. *Oxford Review of Education*

test point. It is difficult to understand the justification for placing the teaching profession, dedicated to working for all students to perform at their best, praising achievement and extra effort, in this dilemma in which too much progress at an early stage might actually penalise schools.

Davies et al. (2005), amongst others, recognised some factors which had led to improvement in examination results and sometimes league table position. Some of these involved curriculum manipulation, for example increasing the number of subjects taken and choosing to accredit more areas of the curriculum. Other possibilities included changing examination boards or subjects to those regarded as 'easier' and focusing on those students on the C/D borderline. Mansell (2007) highlights the GNVQ Intermediate examination, with its potential for students to achieve 4 A*-C grades as one 'shortcut to league table success'. He refers to an Academy, linked with Thomas Telford School, for which the 2005 league table indicated 67% 5A*-C grades in GCSE or equivalent. He points out that if the 'equivalence' were excluded, only 7% had reached 5A*-C.[36] The effect on such inflation on FFT estimates of achievement is clear. Since, to date, FFT B or D estimates have been based on what students at any given level have achieved, those achieving GNVQ Intermediate qualifications are helping artificially to inflate national expectations.

Headteachers in the survey had adopted at least some of the strategies Davies et al. noted although most had not believed that GNVQ whole cohort entry was a justifiable response. One headteacher commented that if all Oxfordshire schools had followed Thomas Telford School's lead, life for the headteachers would have been much easier, since the Local Authority would have been happy with the statistics, irrespective of the skew to the

---

[36] Mansell Warwick, Education by Numbers: The Tyranny of Testing. Politico's 2007 p120

curriculum. Curriculum changes and the targeting of individuals or groups were common. The least changes had occurred in schools with 'better' intakes where good results could be relied upon. Governors and staff were together more able to take risks to support curriculum packages which would best suit the needs of the students but did not necessarily produce level 2 qualifications (GCSE equivalence) or indeed any accreditation. In these cases, such students requiring alternative curriculum models were relatively few. Yet even these schools were refining their curriculum to some extent to meet increasing external demands and in recognition of the need to keep 'improving'.

Schools in more challenging circumstances had made the most changes, taking up more vocational or BTEC Level 2 courses, decreasing the number of students entered only for Entry Level, ensuring that the vast majority of students were entered for 5A*-G including English and maths, and increasingly bearing in mind that entry for less than 8 GCSEs would affect CVA scores. However, all were aware that for some young people, such adjustments were unrealistic or inappropriate and most, particularly when not under extreme pressure to improve KS4 statistics, were prepared to forgo the statistics for the sake of the individual child. In schools with 5A*-C percentages in excess of 60%, there were often a few students who would not be taking 8 GCSEs or the equivalent.

The Headmasters and Headmistresses Conference, (2004) in advice to parents, warns that "league tables encourage schools to 'play safe' where the curriculum is concerned. They create a temptation for schools to:

- adopt a narrow style of teaching (even cramming) to 'teach to the test' – rigid instruction purely to achieve high exam results, rather than encouraging the development of intellectual curiosity or wider practical skills;
- cut down the number of exams taken;

- cut down the General Studies provision to concentrate on exam subjects;
- reduce the extra-curricular provision in such areas as games, music and drama;
- pressure staff and pupils into focussing exclusively on academic matters, with pastoral and wider provision being reduced as a result."[37]

Comparative value-added scores are not specifically useful to schools or to individuals. The time and effort spent by schools on analysis and strategies relating to test results and league tables as they affect the public face of education is important in relation to the schools' standing in their communities. Headteachers know that failure to pay any attention to them may disadvantage their schools and their capacity to assist students, and in particular the most vulnerable students. Headteachers emphasised that internally, however, value added scores may be particularly useful to schools in providing a way of monitoring and tracking individual students and planning further developments on the basis of the analysis.

The importance of the research on league tables for schools which have higher proportions of disadvantaged and vulnerable students is the conclusion that despite much effort and improvement over time, schools in challenging circumstances could not in most cases be expected to achieve for any length of time in the 'significantly higher' categories and it would probably be unreasonable to expect them to do so. That is not to say that they cannot achieve significant improvement, but that factors affecting students' ability to learn and to concentrate on their learning need to be taken into account. While league tables exist, schools will always feature at the bottom of them, but they may be good schools, nevertheless. "Since value-added scores are calculated relative to the national

---

[37] Headmasters and Headmistresses Conference (HMC) (2004) School League Tables What they tell you…and what they don't. *Advice to Parents and Other Interested Parties Information* Page 4-5

average, not all schools can improve."[38] (Ray, 2006 Durrant, 2007) – There will always be schools below average, but they too may be becoming more successful.

Some headteachers believed that the relentless pressure, often made worse by local press reports, led to an inevitable emphasis on 'C/D borderline students' to the detriment of others. 81% of schools in the survey confirmed that in subjects which were set by ability, subject leaders would take care to ensure that Year 9 borderline Level 4/5 sets and KS4 C/D borderline sets would be allocated good teachers. While other sets might well have good teachers too, the priority is clear and the implications of this for some vulnerable students can be drawn. Most schools cannot afford to take risks with the statistics they know matter the most to those in positions of power and influence. If they did, the whole community would suffer. Furthermore, the pass/fail perception of GCSE grades had increased pressures on students and made some students feel their efforts were not valued and were futile. Their worth in education was seen to rest entirely on academic results. Woods and Levacic (2002) note similar observations made in interviews with students and teachers:

> "We've always tried to keep a balance between the development of the child and academic results. But now we need to change the balance. Now we are putting more pressure on them, the behaviour is getting worse." (a teacher with 20 years experience, rated 'good' by students)[39]

73% of the Oxfordshire headteachers surveyed had received some additional funding which was targeted at addressing the needs of

---

[38] Ray, Andrew (2006) School Value Added Measures in England. A Paper for the OECD Project on the Development of Value-Added Models in Education Systems. Department for Education and Skills
[39] Levacic, Rosalind and Woods, Philip A (2002) Raising School Performance in the League Tables Part 2 Barriers to responsiveness in three disadvantaged schools. *British Education Research Journal* 28 No 2 p239

students judged to be performing on the C/D borderline or on the KS3 Level 4/5 borderline. Funding came largely from the Specialist School Trust or from the Local Authority. The latter had initiated the 2+3 project, targeted at achieving C grades in English and maths and three other subjects. Schools themselves had chosen to adopt various strategies including more mock papers, lunchtime and after-school revision and catch-up sessions, mentoring and Easter holiday revision classes, if necessary funding these themselves. Headteachers acknowledged the dangers both in concentrating efforts on these particular students and by default leaving those not working at this grade boundary to feel neglected. They were in fact keen to point out that the school had targeted a number of different groups, for example gifted and talented students, students with poor literacy skills, vulnerable students, students aiming at L6+ at KS3 etc. Some emphasised that the extra sessions, designed for C/D borderline students, were in fact open to all. In other words, they were well aware of the danger of alienating staff, parents and students by an undue emphasis on the C/D borderline. Many were clear that the principles of inclusion and equal opportunities could not and would not be compromised. Again this might be seen to be a more courageous position for schools in which headline percentages based on league tables were an ongoing issue, but most headteachers felt strongly about this. Some headteachers were clear that raising the headline percentage was a means of keeping Ofsted, the Local Authority or even the press happy or 'off my back' in order to proceed with the broader agenda of providing an 'all-round education which addressed the five outcomes of the Every Child Matters agenda, and which would provide students with different kinds of success, skill and self-confidence.

UNICEF indicates that while there are wide variations in educational disadvantage amongst the OECD countries,

"high absolute standards of educational achievement are not incompatible with low levels of relative disadvantage – i.e. the best educational systems allow high-achieving pupils to fulfil their potential whist not allowing others to fall too far behind."[40]

Targets for individual students based on prior attainment do not take into account what may befall the student between one test and another. Given the kinds of social influences and family pressures which impact upon teenagers, uniform progress cannot be assured, especially for those who are vulnerable. Moreover a student who achieved Level 4 in English and maths at KS3 with a reading age of 10, is not likely to make satisfactory progress at KS3 or KS4 if the reading age does not maintain progress in line with their chronological age. These literacy issues may create a further group of vulnerable students in secondary schools, who become more disaffected as the potential for further learning and progress is perceived to drop away. A recognition of the importance of reading ages is to be found in the headteachers' survey in which 70% of the schools were testing all Year 7 students' reading ages on entry. Two schools were testing all students each year to check on progress. It could be argued that primary and secondary schools should be free to focus more specifically on reading ability, since this alone is clearly related to achievement across the subject range, including maths. More work needs to be done here, because such disadvantage will not only be responsible for under-achievement, but may also account for some alienation during the last few years of compulsory education and into adult life. As the UNICEF Report (2007) makes clear:

"Those with low skills and few qualifications face a steepening incline of disadvantage."[41]

Current policies of accountability were therefore perceived by some headteachers to have an effect on the disadvantaged and vulnerable. An emphasis on literacy levels in some schools and a

---

[40] UNICEF Report Card 4 (2002) - (ref in Report Card 7 P20)
[41] UNICEF Report Card 7 (2007) Child poverty in perspective: An overview of child well-being in rich countries.

recognition of the growing numbers of students with English as an additional language arriving throughout secondary school education will properly influence provision and the degree of personalised learning available. One school, recognising the needs of individuals arriving into different year groups throughout the year with little or no English, was providing a GCSE course in five subjects in the Sixth Form. This was an obvious progression route and welcomed by students and their parents. In terms of personalised learning, it was an example of good practice. However, it did not assist the school in terms of league tables for 16 year olds.

Some of the headteachers commented that, despite external pressure on 5A*-C, 5A*G was, in their view, a more important target. They and their staff had put their efforts into raising the level of basic qualifications and were pleased with their success in this area. They expressed regret and frustration that Ofsted and local and national government did not seem to appreciate the significance of this figure in relation to the well-being of society and did not sufficiently recognise the work in these areas which often involved hours of effort by teachers and other staff to support an individual student.   Such views reflect the opinions of the teachers and headteachers interviewed by Woods and Levacic (2002)[42] It is interesting to note that, despite well publicised figures of almost 300,000 young people leaving with few or no GCSE qualifications and the growing NEET numbers, the 5A*-G percentage is, from 2009, no longer a compulsory target.

Throughout such steeplechases towards prizes for academic achievement, the casualties may therefore be seen to be both the individual vulnerable young people and the schools with higher percentages of disadvantaged and vulnerable students. For some, the relentless pursuit towards academic excellence falls at the first

---

[42] Levacic, Rosalind and Woods, Philip A Raising School Performance in the League Tables Part 2 Barriers to responsiveness in three disadvantaged schools. *British Education Research Journal* 2002 28 No 2 p 239

hurdle with poor literacy skills; for others the race is attempted but, given their deficit and lack of support from home, the effort is too great or the demands excessive.

Since it is in the interests both of the government and the local authorities to galvanise schools into producing higher and higher test results, it is difficult for schools to question the assumptions on which such an approach is based, without appearing defensive or complacent. Certainly, it would appear that average national achievement within categories has been inflated by, for example, the entry of whole cohorts in GNVQ Intermediate examinations, worth 4 GCSEs. As discussed above, it is possible that over-achievement in this way has pushed FFT estimates of achievement to unrealistic levels for schools not engaged in such courses. However, as more schools investigate different kinds of courses which will keep their statistics away from unwanted attention, it is to be hoped that the figures are not driving the curriculum (as it appears to have done in the case of Modern Foreign Languages) and that students are still able to benefit from a broad and balanced education. The most recent measure, 5A*-C including English and maths, is designed to adjust balance in the measure of achievement, but in fact leads to an overemphasis on another part of the curriculum (i.e. maths).

It may be that the 14-19 developments are timely and should provide for more progression, and greater flexibility, at a pace appropriate to the learner. Once more the government needs to resist the notion that one size fits all and phrases like 'the qualification of choice' do not sit well with a commitment to personalized learning. GCSEs, BTECs, A levels, IB and the new Diploma courses may all play a part in ensuring that young people will be excited and stimulated by new opportunities to learn, will improve basic skills and will grow in confidence knowing that they are successful and have a contribution to make to the community.

It has been necessary here to look at the whole-scale effects of policies relating to targets, testing and league tables because vulnerable students, as all young people, are affected by the ability of their schools to assist them in making progress and to answer their needs. It is clear that at present academic achievement in the higher levels is a driving force which does not recognize sufficiently the achievement of those making progress at lower levels. Schools find themselves engaging in increasing numbers of initiatives in order to raise test and examination performance within certain categories and to do so at a number of well-defined stages. Such considerations contradict the principles of personalized learning and do not enable vulnerable students and lower achievers to believe that they matter. Schools are working hard to provide equal opportunities for all their students but the pressures of current policies do not assist them.

SUCCESS

"Youngsters have always been awkward when they feel themselves to be unsuccessful.........We are trying to develop provision and a curriculum option that enables them to cope."

"When GCSE was introduced there was no talk of pass/fail. Now that is used routinely – there is a sense of failure."

"We have focused on all grades being measures of achievement, not failure."

Success according to a dictionary definition is 'the favourable outcome of something attempted' (Collins). In educational terms it may be seen as the positive recognition of achievement. Students sit their examinations each year and achieve levels and grades. If they achieve in line with their predicted level or grade or surpass it, or if they overcome difficulties and make significant progress, they are successful, and their success should be recognized. There are also many other kinds of achievement which need similar recognition. In any learning institution the celebration of success must play a major role if motivation is to be sustained. Equally, if schools are to produce successful citizens who have a pride in, and an ownership of their place of learning, and who will sustain an interest in learning throughout their lives, they need praise and encouragement and opportunities to have their successes acknowledged. If schools are providing good quality education and establishing an ethos in which learning is promoted and skills, talents and interests nurtured and developed, they too need their many achievements publicly recognized and rewarded.

A student's success in one aspect of life can affect others as confidence builds and students are mentally ready to take on other challenges. Criteria-referenced goals are often used with students because this kind of assessment is clear for students and they know exactly what they have to do to achieve the goal. There are many examples of these kinds of assessment – for example, the Youth Award scheme (ASDAN), the National Vocational Qualifications (NVQ) framework for vocational areas and the Duke of Edinburgh Award Scheme. Many of the behaviour modification and pastoral support programmes are built on this system, where goals or targets are clear, precise and achievable and in which the competition is in personal challenge. Through such programmes, students also learn how to recognise and acknowledge the success of others. Those working with these assessments know that encouragement and praise, when praise is due, motivates and raises self-esteem. This is supported by a study into ways in which effective schools raised boys' attainment (Lindsay & Muijs 2006)

> "These schools had high, but realistic, expectations of their students. They also placed emphasis on achievement in extra-curricular areas and displays and rewards were used to celebrate achievement… Competing for awards had a particularly marked effect on boys' motivation"[43]

Studies have shown that a more positive self-image is linked to high achievement for both girls and boys. Mitchell and Hiron (2002)[44] found that high achieving girls expressed realistic confidence in their forthcoming examinations, but lower achieving boys had a more negative self-image in relation to other boys. Such a low self-image was the result of years of reinforcement of 'failure' and little experience or recognition of success.

> "At the age of 16, students in England have undergone a battery of tests and are arguably equipped with more performance data than ever before. It is less likely that they can escape the reality of their current academic status."

---

[43] Lindsay G, Muijs D, (2006) Challenging underachievement in boys. *Educational Research* 48 (3) pp 313-332

[44] Mitchell, Graham Hirom, Kate (2002) The role of explanatory style in the academic underperformance of boys. European Conference on Educational Research, Lisbon 11-14 p9

Since, in inspections conducted in 2007-2008, target-setting and students awareness of their targets are emphasised, this statement is probably an accurate reflection on current practice. Students arrive from primary school knowing that they are 'a Level 4' or 'a Level 3'(Reay and Wiliam 1999). In many secondary schools, targets, including predicted levels and grades, are written in exercise books or homework planners and shared with parents on a regular basis. Moreover it is clear that the style for learning in most secondary schools is less person-centred than in primary schools. So "because of the reduced emphasis on the individual, the differences between these two states –success and failure– is more strongly focused."

Most headteachers did not believe that academic targets were in themselves detrimental, but they were concerned that they were realistic and were used for the right purposes i.e. to raise expectations and improve students' motivation. For the well motivated individual, they provided a realistic goal, which motivated a student and when achieved, would provide a reason for celebration and a raising of self-esteem. FFTD whole school targets were generally accepted as aspirational, if sometimes unrealistic, but useful in raising expectations of staff and sometimes of students. However, some headteachers expressed concern that if tables were produced which show actual results against FFTD estimates, as opposed to the statutory targets set by the governors of their schools, then up to 75% of their schools were being set up for 'failure', by the nature of the set of estimates (FFTD) on which targets had been based. This is of specific importance to schools in challenging circumstances, in which many of the factors which relate to disadvantaged and vulnerable students and which are not taken into account by FFTD figures, will affect performance. It follows then that even for schools which had improved their results and met the statutory targets, publicity would be negative and success turned to failure.

Teachers arrive in the profession determined to enthuse their students with a desire for learning, and to provide opportunities for success and achievement. They are required to raise expectations and aspirations and know the importance of so doing. Teachers do not normally seek to improve an individual's performance by branding them 'a failure' – they may well suggest that a test result is poor, that the student could do better, or make more effort – such individual feedback is not for public consumption but for individual reflection, and will be accompanied by advice or encouragement. They are to remember that the ratio of praise to blame should be at least 3:1. All teachers will also be aware that they are urged, when facing poor behaviour, to condemn the behaviour but never the person. These are clearly important principles, particularly when students are vulnerable, unfamiliar with praise and often regarded at school and at home as 'difficult'.

One of the ways in which contradictions in present educational policy manifest themselves is in the choice of vocabulary in the official documentation. Ofsted notes that some significant strengths in practice have been seen which have 'countered the effects of disadvantage'. The first of four factors mentioned as fundamental to such practice was 'belief on the part of staff that all learners, whatever their circumstances, can and should achieve success.'[45] However, the language in which the report is couched in the preceding pages hardly adheres to the principle so clearly stated as fundamental to the learning process. For example, in commenting on deprived pupils in terms of free school meal measures, the report states:

> "…it remains the case that schools with high proportions of pupils from deprived backgrounds are more likely to be inadequate than those serving more affluent communities."[46]

---

[45] The Annual Report of Her Majesty's Chief Inspector 2006-7 p 74
[46] Ibid. P 65

If all schools and all staff are to believe that they can and should achieve success, then words such as 'inadequate' do not promote the encouraging and optimistic approach which teachers are expected to adopt. A specific problem is here translated into a label for the school as a whole.

In the previous framework, the extent to which schools were meeting the demands of the Every Child Matters agenda, in relation to the Five Outcomes, was specifically reported. Of the schools in Special Measures at the end of August 2007, 70% were agreed by Ofsted to be succeeding across the board in every category of four of the five outcomes, the very values which society increasingly emphasises as essential for young people to learn.[47] (See Appendix 2) It is interesting to note that this form of report has now ceased. Therefore, in four of the five categories of the Every Child Matters agenda, a school labelled 'failing' was regarded as at least a satisfactory school.[48] In addition, some of the schools which had been placed in Special Measures also had satisfactory judgements on other criteria such as work in partnership with others to promote learners' well-being; equality of opportunity promoted and discrimination tackled so that all learners achieve as well as they can in school; how well the curriculum and other activities met the range of needs and interests of learners; the extent of learners' spiritual, moral, social and cultural development; how well learners are cared for, guided and supported and the behaviour of learners. The fifth outcome 'Enjoy and Achieve' could also have been met by some of these schools. Students might be enjoying their education and achieving in different ways; clearly they were not achieving certain expected academic results. That schools may have needed advice, guidance and additional support is possible and, with such assistance, results might well improve. That they should be 'penalised' so heavily by being labelled as a 'failing school' is at least open to question.

---

[47] Ofsted Inspection Report 2005-2006 Annex B
[48] This particular grid was dropped from the documentation for the inspections from September 2006.

Since success in standards requires the confidence of the local community to continue to send to the school students with a broad range of ability and social background, such labelling on the basis of examination results alone might be regarded as a self-fulfilling prophecy.

Secondary headteachers interviewed in this study recognised the narrowing focus of judgments on success, and the direction in which the standards agenda was taking schools. They held to a broader definition of success, often reflected in the school's Self-Evaluation Form and Prospectus, together with publications to parents and the community, but felt this was not always recognised, particularly by Ofsted. Some resented the message that if judgments on standards, which they believed were centred largely on the 5A*-C percentage with and without English and maths, were 'only' satisfactory, judgements on leadership and management and on teaching and learning for the school as a whole were likely to be no more than satisfactory. Thus judgments on the school's success overall, in the text of an Ofsted report, were skewed to a range of specific examination results. The Inspection did not fairly reflect ways in which the school as a whole was perceived to be successfully delivering the five outcomes of the Every Child Matters agenda. Some also saw a difference between what was written in the report, which was often positive and complimentary, and the grade (often a 3) awarded and judged that this too was also a result of an undue emphasis on 'standards'.

Statements about failing individuals or failing schools are destructive. A school which is providing an effective education as judged by most of the Five Outcomes for children, but is not achieving the academic targets set or the Contextual Value-Added expected, is not a failing school. It may be a successful school in which students are achieving well – it may be that it is not being as successful in, say maths, as it should be according to national statistics. Similarly, a teacher whose lesson is judged to be 'inadequate' is not a failing teacher - unless all lessons are inadequate. There may be weaknesses in teaching or learning but these will not be better addressed by the use of such negative language.

During 2007 a number of headteachers of independent and public schools voiced concern about the direction education appears to be taking. Of league tables, some have been very critical - "'They tell us nothing at all about the other important things a good school provides – the culture, sport, leadership, care and discipline."[49] Martin Stephen, Headteacher of St Paul's School, was reported to be considering withdrawing his school from the league tables. He described them as 'a cancer on the face of education'. He also remarked that schools in the lowest 30% of the tables did not receive credit for the good work they were doing. "League tables… have delivered education into the hands of the media."[50]

All the headteachers interviewed were keen to emphasise that achievement in all areas of school life was celebrated - rewards and prizes were offered, and special evenings arranged. Media coverage, exhibitions of activities, newsletters and website entries ensured that students had opportunities to be praised for their efforts and success to be recognised and rewarded. This success was not by any means for academic performance alone. Student success was celebrated in the performing arts, in work-related contexts, in productions, charity events, sports teams, outdoor education, individual competitions, residential opportunities at home and abroad, in gaining young apprenticeship places, Duke of Edinburgh awards and many other achievements. Display in corridors and foyers focused on a wide range of achievement, involving a cross-section of the school community in age, ability and talent across a wide range of activities.

---

[49] Witheridge John, Headmaster of Charterhouse Daily Telegraph 25th August 2007

[50] Stephen Martin Headmaster of St Paul's School London Times Educational Supplement 30th November 2007

Vulnerable young people are entitled to experience success in their education. When they achieve, they expect their effort and their achievement to be recognized. Education provides for growth in many ways and in different contexts. Not all young people will gain high academic grades, but if their education is a positive experience and their progress acknowledged as success, they will discover their strengths, reflect on their priorities and develop spiritual, moral social and cultural insights. They and their parents need opportunities to celebrate such success and they need to know that their school is successful – that they belong to an institution of which they can be proud and whose success they will continue to support in the years to come.

ENCOURAGEMENT

SELF-ESTEEM

"Our nurture group in Year 7 raises self-esteem and helps manage behaviour. Reducing the number of teachers involved helps this."

"Low self-esteem, poor motivation and a poor learning environment contribute to disadvantage and underachievement."

Headteachers emphasised the importance of raising self-esteem, particularly amongst vulnerable young people. Such students had often experienced failure and could sometimes be motivated by special attention (e.g.mentoring), identification as someone who was worth targeting (e.g. membership of a special group) or success in one aspect of school life (e.g. sport, performing arts). Residential experience also raised self-esteem but often, vulnerable students, whose parents might be able to contribute financially to such an experience, or who were offered a free place, did not have the self-confidence or sufficiently robust relationships with peers to want to risk a residential experience from which they could not easily withdraw. Headteachers interviewed were aware of the motivational power of praise and of a reward system valued by their students. They also knew that building confidence and a more robust self-image was a significant factor both in raising achievement and enabling vulnerable students to regard achievement as success.

A study of developmental causes of disaffection (N Humphrey et al., 2004) found that "pupils of low ability were more likely to be depressed and have low levels of self-esteem than their more able peers"[51] While high achieving pupils rated behaviour and conduct to be a feature in their education, low achievers thought that academic competence, social acceptance, athletic competence and physical appearance were more important. Academic competence was "significantly more likely to be a negative source of self-esteem for low achieving pupils." (Humphrey et al., 2004)[52]

The National Curriculum, and the assessments associated with it, has had a poor affect on some students' self-esteem. A study undertaken by Harlen and Deakin Crick (2002)[53] found that 'repeated practice prior to tests, tended to reinforce the poor self-image of the lower achievers', given that each time, they were faced with evidence of their poor achievement compared with others. Harlen and Deakin Crick (2002) reported:

> 'After the introduction of the National Curriculum Tests in England, low achieving pupils had lower self-esteem than higher-achieving pupils, whilst there was no correlation between self-esteem and achievement prior to this.'

It is perhaps not surprising that a number of studies (Humphrey, 2004; Riley and Rustique Forrester et al., 2002) indicate that low achieving pupils, faced with the prospect of academic failure and its effect of their self esteem, choose to engage in more rewarding areas or subcultures and that this phenomenon can be seen at the beginning of an individual's secondary education, if not the end of their primary education (c.f. Furlong, 1991; Kinder, 1997). Mitchell and Hiron (2002) comment:

---

[51] Humphreys Neil, Newton Irene, Charlton John P (2004) The developmental roots of disaffection. *Educational Psychology* 24 (5) pp579-594 P591
[52] Ibid p 589
[53] Harlen, W. & Deakin Crick, R. (2002). A systematic review of the impact of summative assessment and tests on students' motivation for learning. London: EPPI-Centre, Social Science Research Unit, Institute of Education.

"If examination performances are the only public measures of the worth of an individual, it is not surprising that some will look elsewhere for success or self-esteem"[54]

National Curriculum tests (SATs) are claimed to be for the benefit of parents and children in assessing standards; in reality their major use is the provision of data on the performance of schools within a market culture. In fact parents and students do not need to rely on these results to indicate progress at school but expect annual reports and progress reports from class teachers to provide such information. Reay and Wiliam (1999) conducted research with Year 6 students over the months prior to their SATs at the end of KS2. It was clear that the tests were a major focus for work throughout Year 6 and that the anxieties of the teachers were being passed on to the children. Researchers noted sharp currents of fear and anxiety on the part of Year 6 pupils. Examples of responses showing pupils' views on these tests were revealing:

A".....you have to get a level like a level 4 or a level 5 and if you're no good at spellings or times tables you don't get these levels and so you're a nothing."
Q: "If you get a level two, what will that say about you?'
A:" Um, I might not have a good life in front of me and I might grow up and do something naughty or something like that."[55]

Clarke (1997) [56], a former Oxfordshire headteacher, provides a similar illustration of the problem in a secondary school in an incident in which a 16 year old was sent to him for being extremely rude to a teacher. He had been very rude. The boy had been given a

[54] Mitchell, Graham Hirom, Kate (2002) The role of explanatory style in the academic underperformance of boys. European Conference on Educational Research, Lisbon 11-14 P 10
[55] Reay Diane, Wiliam Dylan(1999) 'I'll be a nothing': structure, agency and the construction of identity through assessment. *British Educational Research Journal* 25 (3) pp343-354
[56] Clarke Bernard (1997) in Affirming the Comprehensive Ideal. London, Palmer ed Pring, R and Walford G

G grade for a piece of homework. He had spent much time on the work. He had visited the library. He had even missed watching Oxford United play an important match, but his effort had been given a G. His friend who had spent much less time and had written one side of paper received an A. He told his headteacher, 'I hate Gs!' He felt a sense of hopelessness and confidence in his ability to achieve was diminished. His self-esteem was low and he had become frustrated and angry.

Some headteachers noted concern from their staff about too much emphasis on the target grades to those at the lower end of the ability range. However, teachers wanted to be encouraging - they would set a low target, based on performance and data estimates, but they would be encouraging. They needed to emphasise that an F was a pass grade and would give students points. One student, engaged in a mentor session with his headteacher was asked about his targets for different subjects. He replied in a pleasant but resigned tone "They are mostly Fs and Gs. I'm quite thick, you know. Do you want me to go through them one by one?' The headteacher declined. Concern about the sharing of targets had also occasionally been expressed by parents, but this arose from parents who felt that a target grade of C lowered the sights of their more able children. Conversations with parents of vulnerable young people tended to address more immediate issues of concern, often behaviour or curriculum arrangements, but parents were often aware of their son or daughter's low expectations and aspirations.

A report by the Mental Health Foundation[57] indicated that the desire to 'raise standards' may be contributing to statistics that suggest that one in five pupils suffers from anxiety or worse and that the numbers of those suffering from depression, anxiety or psychosis are increasing. Lovey comments:

---

[57] Mental Health Foundation reported in TES 25 June 1999 P12

"It is not surprising to learn that the negative impact of a narrowly focused academic definition of raising standards can be seen in recent research showing increased pupil distress in primary school and of new pressures in secondary schools."[58]

Mitchell and Hirom[59] interviewed students in three Northamptonshire comprehensives schools specifically looking at how explanatory style was being used by boys and girls to provide reasons for negative and positive school experiences. They studied statements which referred to explanations for events which were external (relating to other people or circumstances), unstable (a one-off event) and specific (just relating to this experience) together with explanations which were internal (relating to the student themselves), stable (likely to be present in the future) and global (influencing other areas of the student's life). So optimistic explanatory style used to explain bad events would be external, unstable and specific and pessimistic explanatory style to explain bad events would be internal, stable and global. The research indicated that patterns of academic success had helped to build high levels of optimism and self-esteem and that these levels built up as more success was achieved. Students knew how well they were doing and this would affect the degree of effort as they got older. Boys' lack of effort (e.g. 'I like mucking about' (global)) was often mentioned as a reason for lack of success, a possible 'useful defensive strategy' which could provide a reason for boys not asking for help and for being demotivated. The study went on to suggest that it was possible that effective mentors, if trained, could modify such explanatory style to produce one which raised self-esteem and fitted better into a pattern for academic achievement and enjoyment.

---

[58] Lovey Jane (2000) *Disengagement, Truancy and Exclusion.* in Ed Docking Jim New Labour's Policies for Schools Raising the Standard? David Fulton London
[59] Mitchell, Graham Hirom, Kate (2002) *The role of explanatory style in the academic underperformance of boys* European Conference on Educational Research, Lisbon 11-14

It is not difficult to appreciate that all young people benefit from individual attention. Certainly headteachers believed that mentoring, put in place largely for Year 11 students on the C/D borderline, was successful to the extent that the mentors enabled one to one conversations which raised the profile of the work students were undertaking and offered them some time individually. Approximately 50% of the headteachers, referring to strategies to raise achievement, specifically mentioned mentoring in some form, often involving members of staff and the senior leadership team and sometimes including mentors from the community. It is clear from various studies (Riley and Rustique Forrester, 2002; Searle, 2005; Hilton, 2006) that vulnerable young people particularly value and need such attention. Students often feel that they want to talk to someone, but no one has time to listen (Riley and Rustique Forrester, 2002 p57) and key workers at Pupil Referral Units provided this kind of support. Headteachers supported the research findings here - that the quality of the relationships established is crucial to the progress which can be made. (Solomon and Rogers, 2001)

Lovey (2000) writes of a previous study (Lovey et al., 1993) when the proactive placement of Year 10 pupils in college courses and the provision of well thought-out work experience which involved skills training was seen to have a marked effect on behaviour and attendance. She comments, "There must be a pathway... ...where all can achieve some success and upon which those tired of education can build later, when they have recovered the self-esteem that has been robbed from them because of failure in an overtly academic curriculum"[60]. Headteachers reported similar results with good behaviour and improved attendance noted both in the placements at College or on work experience and also within lessons back in school on the remaining days of the week. Students were experiencing success, they were regaining control of their

---

[60] Lovey Jane (2000) *Disengagement, Truancy and Exclusion* Ch.12 in New Labour's Policies for Schools ed J Docking page 201

future and their self-esteem was rising. For all involved, their success was crucial. Whether they achieve Level 1 or Level 2 qualifications by the end of Year 11 was less important, because progression was available post-16. Headteachers felt that the priority had to be the needs of the individual student, yet in terms of value-added scores and league tables, that decision had a consequence for the school unconnected with the interests of the individual.

Just as students need praise and encouragement in order to sustain self-esteem and make progress, so do schools. A study of the effect of league tables on schools in Scotland (Croxford 1999) concluded "The policy of publishing league tables is based on the perception that 'naming and shaming' schools will bring about school improvement. There is no evidence that this policy is effective. In fact the publication of league tables is detrimental to schools."[61] Such views are also expressed by Reed and Hallgarten (2003)[62] and in a Guardian leader "There is no doubt whatsoever that performance tables, in the current form are damaging the educational health of low achievers." (cit. Searle 2001 p116)

The culture of the 'School Improvement' campaign runs directly in opposition to the strategies recommended to improve student learning. Teachers understand that an ethos which supports learning for students requires high but realistic expectations and much encouragement and praise. This in turn enhances motivation and empowers young people to take control and make the best of their opportunities. For staff in schools, this approach is a way of life; every day is treated as a new day, grudges are not carried over, weaknesses and mistakes are discussed, analysed and all move on; students are not put down, humiliated, bullied or threatened.

---

[61] Croxford Linda, (1999) League tables: who needs them? *CES Briefing Centre for Educational Sociology* No 14 pp4

[62] Jodie Reed and Joe Hallgarten (2003) Time to say goodbye? The future of school performance tables www.leeds.ac.uk/educol/documents/00003500.htm P8

However, the language in which both reforms and accountability measures have been couched has followed very different principles. Schools with perceived 'weaknesses' will be punished. The language is routinely of a blame culture and is threatening – phrases such as 'a school of concern', 'inadequate', 'notice to improve', 'special measures'. Warnings are made public, threats of being closed or taken over are common and grants are withheld or provided with conditions. Parents are told in the press that 'X is a failing school'. It should come as a surprise to no one when the headlines read 'middle classes abandon state schools'[63] or 'pupils take flight from bad schools'[64] when there is such relentless thoughtlessness. There are many 'own goals' and once the local authority, or Ofsted, or the government make statements using this kind of negative language, others are left to pick up the pieces and repair the damage. (Barton (2007 p9))[65] Local reputations built up carefully over a number of years may be destroyed in a matter of weeks.

There is also an unhelpful gap between the interpretation of certain key words by professionals and their understanding by parents, local communities and the press. Thus Ofsted inspectors inform staff personally in schools that 'satisfactory' is equivalent to the previous judgement of 'good' – a reassurance which manifestly fails to console when the definition of 'satisfactory' in the documentation remains 'inadequate in no major respect, maybe good in some respects.' Durrant (2007) points out the contradictions in the use of language by Ofsted. He makes the point that if the Oxford English Dictionary defines satisfactory as 'adequate: leaving no room for complaint', "it is therefore nonsense to express dissatisfaction with 'satisfactory' schools. If a school is 'satisfactory', then that must mean that the school is

---

[63] Daily Telegraph 10th November 2007
[64] Sunday Telegraph 18th November 2007
[65] Barton G (2007) Shouldn't Ofsted by helping us to improve our schools? National Education Trust

'good enough'."[66]. No headteacher, even of a school performing well, was complacent; all were aware of developments which were needed or issues which required more attention. Some however expressed frustration that real gain and positive achievement were not recognized and the emphasis remained on 'not good enough.'

Thus the blame culture affects teachers as well as students. A report published in 2007[67] records 19% of secondary schools, 35% primary schools and 33% of special schools failing to appoint a new headteacher. Headteachers believe that leading a school is an exciting and challenging prospect but if the rewards are few and the position is too precarious or stress-ridden, then it is not surprising that fewer teachers are prepared to take up or sustain their enthusiasm for such posts in maintained schools. The low self-esteem of teachers also has an effect. Both young teachers entering the profession and teachers with more experience are normally self-critical and keen to analyse their own performance. Yet they do not want to be told their work is 'inadequate' because they have not shown in a lesson how much students have learnt. Much less do they appreciate one 'inadequate' – styled lesson leading to a conclusion about their competence as 'an inadequate teacher.' Encouraging staff to be creative becomes more difficult in a climate where formulaic teaching is seen to be advocated and rewarded. The training of more Special Educational Needs teachers has to be a high priority when so many students need their expertise. High quality teaching is crucial for student progress, and not least in areas of greatest deprivation, where high level skills are arguably most needed, but current policies, including targets, testing and league tables militate against this. Teachers fear that their careers may be blighted by association with a 'failing' school or that the pressures of working in such a school, a combination of

---

[66] Durrant Danny (2007) *The role of UK Local Authorities to support school improvement.* Paper presented at the British Educational research Association Annual Conference, p 14

[67] Howson, John: (2007) *13th Annual Survey of the Labour Market for Senior Staff in Schools across England and Wales*

government policy and other external pressures, will put them under too much strain to achieve a work-life balance.

The greatest incentives for teachers are trust and freedom to operate as a professional educator. Smithers and Robinson (2002)[68], investigating the reasons why teachers leave the profession, found that only 53 out of every hundred persons are still in teaching after three years. The most significant reasons for this were workload, new challenges and the school situation. The current difficulties in recruitment and particularly retention of headteachers and other staff indicate that salary is not the major driving force here. Smithers and Robinson (2003) cite another survey by Edmonds, Sharp and Benefield (2002): "They found that people tend to be drawn to teaching by intrinsic occupational values such as wanting to work with children, search for intellectual fulfilment and the sense of contributing to society"[69]. Appropriate work-life balance, the opportunity to make a difference to the lives of young people, flexibility to match curriculum and pace to the needs of individuals and the belief that a career could not be damaged by a risk-taking move, are seen to be more important factors than salary. These findings are supported by the McKinsey Report (2007) [70], comparing schools systems across the world, which indicates that the status of the profession needs careful management and cannot be enhanced by salary alone. It concludes that "the quality of an education system cannot exceed the quality of its teachers."

"In all of the systems we studied, the ability of a school system to attract the right people into teaching is closely linked to the status of the profession. In Singapore and South Korea, opinion polls

---

[68] Smithers Alan, Robinson Pamela (2003)*Factors affecting Teachers Decision to leave the Profession*
[69] Edmonds, S, Sharp, C Benefield, P (2002) *Recruitment and Retention on Initial Teacher training: a Systematic Review* Slough NFER cited by Smithers and Robinson.
[70] McKinsey Report (2007) How the world's best performing school systems come out on top.

show that the general public believe that teachers make a greater contribution to society than any other profession."[71]

Headteachers in the survey were committed to their work and proud of their schools. Signs of celebration on a wide range of curricular and extra-curricular success were plain to see around their schools, in classrooms and in publications. They were aware of the importance for their staff and students and for the standing of the school in the community of providing the press with good news stories and there were many of them. Yet those in more challenging circumstances recognised that the demands of coping with league tables and their implications, meeting ever-increasing targets and facing the next inspection were heavy. John Dunford, the general secretary of the Association of School and College Leaders expressed the strain:

> "Too often, ASCL members are just one poor inspection grade away from their P45. Too often ASCL members are sacked precipitately before an Ofsted inspection by nervous local authorities that have previously failed to support the school in its difficulties."[72]

Howson (2007) provides the information that the largest single category cited for the departure of a headteacher was 'retirement before sixty for any reason' (40%)[73] Deaths and illness caused by stress and suicides of school leaders speak for themselves.

Teachers need self-esteem to function effectively. One study (Perryman 2007)[74] detailed responses from teachers about their reactions to the threat of an inspection. They referred to being unable to sleep, spending long hours in school in evenings and

---

[71] Ibid p 22

[72] Richard Garner reporting John Dunford 'Headteachers jobs in danger' The Independent 12th March 2007

[73] Howson John NAHT/ASCL 2007 Annual Survey (June)

[74] Perryman Jane (2007) Inspection and emotion. *Cambridge Journal of Education* 37-2 -173

weekends, panic attacks, fear of special measures and all that this would do to the community, people losing their jobs, senior teachers forced to resign, everyone feeling undervalued. Teachers in schools which are placed in a category as a result of an inspection in schools are subject to immense pressure. One of the schools Perryman studied was subjected to eight inspections in 18 months, and in one phase of this, five inspections in nine months and unsurprisingly found staff were demoralized and exhausted. Staff descriptions of the experience of special measures included phrases such as 'treadmill', 'jumping over hurdles', 'a living hell', and 'a crazy cycle of working like mad followed by a period of near collapse.'[75] In these circumstances, teachers see themselves as a workforce to be managed, not as a profession to be respected for its skills. Many teachers, however committed, will in these circumstances reconsider their position and family members, watching from the sidelines with concern, will also want change. Good teachers, sometimes the most conscientious, leave the profession. Given the evidence that many teachers, on entering the profession, have a vision of making a real difference to the lives of students, they could be encouraged to teach in more challenging schools. However, they need security of tenure and a belief that working in a school which, of its nature, is not going to sit in the top half of a county league table, will not damage their careers or adversely affect their self-esteem, their career or their home-life.

Raising levels of achievement will involve raising self-esteem. Vulnerable students respond well to praise and encouragement and to the provision of opportunities in which they are able to show strengths and talents. Their self-esteem is an important factor in their progress and ultimate success. In the same way, teachers also need self-esteem. If the profession is to retain good teachers whose ability to inspire and enthuse young people can be drawn upon throughout their professional life, it requires support from

---

[75] Perryman Jane (2007) Inspection and emotion. *Cambridge Journal of Education* 37-2 -P 183

government and local authorities to sustain and indeed enhance the status, and thus the self-esteem, of teachers and all those who work in schools.

RESPECT

"All I do is intended to help children achieve, but recent government directives have put children into categories and this is damaging."

"Teachers are less willing to give the time to more troublesome pupils because they distract the teacher and other learners. We are less inclined to give them the time and patience that could bring results. They are increasingly marginalized and this is more common in the new generation of teachers."

Headteachers emphasised the importance of creating an ethos in a school which incorporated a climate of respect. Lack of basic respect for others e.g. hitting another student, making a racist remark, the use of obscene language directed at staff, was often a reason for fixed term exclusions. Fixed term exclusions for specific offences had not been affected by published statistics because these were usually matters of principle, often related to relationships with students or staff, in which the governors and teachers were agreed that a firm stand needed to be made. Some schools, having established specific units or centres to cope with such behaviour, were endeavouring to do more internal exclusion. However, the message to students was clear - respect for others was a basic requirement which could not be compromised.

It is clear that the quality of the relationships experienced in a school affects student engagement and achievement. For some students, the number of different staff they meet in an average day may in itself be a barrier to establishing stability and students should expect to find at least one adult who understands them and will have time for them. This is particularly important for vulnerable students who may have difficulty in making relationships and whose history contributes to their suspicion and distrust of adults. Staff working with students who had been permanently excluded from school understood the importance of their success in establishing these relationships.

Riley and Docking (2004) studied the views of teachers, disaffected students and their parents in two different locations. It was clear that many disaffected students did not dislike school as a whole; they did however dislike certain lessons and would be likely to truant from these. Many wanted to come to school to socialise and to take part in particular activities which they enjoyed e.g. sport. They wanted to be noticed and valued and the quality of care and interest as well as the expertise in teaching was important for them. They also wanted respect as a person in their own right.

> "Pupils wanted to be mentored. Teachers wanted to spend more time with individual students. Parents, pupils and teachers welcomed positive behaviour policies based on mutual respect."[76]

Hilton (2006), following interviews with 40 teenagers who either had been excluded or were truants, underlines the effect of unhappy or unsuccessful relationships experienced throughout the day by these vulnerable students. There was a perception of lack of respect from the teachers and sometimes of an active dislike of them as individuals. They believed they were targeted, judged, labelled, picked on and that some staff had given up on them. This is echoed in other studies:

> "They [students] were very critical of teachers who humiliated them when they were behaving badly – an approach which was seen to exacerbate problems of disrespect and disaffection"[77]

Sometimes they believed sibling behaviour or even a knowledge of their parents when they were at school was affecting the view

---

[76] Riley Kathryn, Docking Jim Voices of Disaffected pupils: Implications for Policy and Practice. *British Journal of Educational Studies* 52 No 2 June 2004 pp 166-179 page 169

[77] Riley & Rustique Forrester 2002 Working with Disaffected students. London, Paul Chapman P175

taken of them. Students in both these studies were clear about the personal qualities of those members of staff who treated them well, like an adult. They wanted to be listened to, encouraged and taken seriously. (Riley and Docking 2004)

> "They mentioned, in particular, teachers who demonstrated friendliness and kindness, listened to pupils' problems and sorted out bullying, treated them fairly while controlling classes in a firm but relaxed manner, praised them for good behaviour, helped them to understand their work and responded readily to individual requests for help."[78]

Good relationships were therefore the key to success. Headteachers emphasised that in making special arrangements for vulnerable children, the personnel available or the kind of person appointed specifically to do such work was a crucial factor in the perceived success of the arrangement (c.f.Riley & Rustique Forrester 2002 p169[79]). Most schools had in place full or part-time counsellors and first aiders / nurses, welfare managers or non-teaching assistant year-leaders who, in addition to the teaching assistants, developed relationships with young people which supported them and their learning. The value of this kind of support is underlined by Vulliamy and Webb (2003) who found that disaffected students and their parents sometimes related well to workers who were not teachers, who were seen to be independent or neutral but were school-based e.g. home-school links workers.[80] Headteachers confirmed that Connexions staff also sometimes fulfilled this kind of mediating role.

---

[78] Riley Kathryn and Docking Jim Docking Jim Voices of Disaffected pupils: Implications for Policy and Practice. *British Journal of Educational Studies* 52 (2) June 2004 pp 166-179 p 175
[79] Riley & Rustique Forrester[79] 2002 Working with Disaffected students. London, Paul Chapman P169
[80] Vulliamy, Graham, Webb, Rosemary (2003) Supporting disaffected pupils: perspectives from the pupils, their parents and their teachers. *Educational Research* 45 (3) 275-286

The recent emphasis on the gathering of students' views on their education and the growing understanding of the need to engage them fully in the learning process are important developments, which should enable each student to be seen as an individual and as such uniquely valuable. Society as a whole recognises the need of individuals for respect to sustain motivation and self-confidence. Ruddock and Flutter (2000) have shown that pupil voice can enhance commitment and motivation[81] but the effectiveness of such engagement rests on respect for students' views.

The development in 2005 in Ofsted reports of letters to the students is an example of an initiative which appears to recognise student voice and which could be used to engage and motivate students in their learning. In some schools however they may fuel a lack of respect. Such letters, which should reflect a recognition of the students active part in and responsibility for learning and accord them respect, are in danger of undermining the respect in which teachers need to be held. Instead of an appropriate opportunity for quality feedback and expert advice, such a letter may become a punitive device, a weapon held against teachers by students and indeed their parents. Letters which celebrate student success and provide guidance on ways they could further develop their learning may be helpful. Letters which include sentences outlining what teachers or headteachers need to improve do not increase respect for those in authority and will not improve student learning, since acting on the recommendations lies, in these cases, beyond the control of the students. Given that students have full access to the whole report, the motive for inclusion of such comments in letters addressed specifically to students must be questionable. The following extracts from Ofsted reports illustrate this lack of respect for the profession which is likely both to undermine authority and impede further progress.

---

[81] Rudduck J and Flutter J (2000) Pupil participation and pupil perspective: 'craving a new order of experience', *Cambridge Journal of Education* 30 No 1 pp 75-89 p 82

"While you benefit from some good lessons, there aren't enough of them and indeed too many of your lessons are unsatisfactory"

"We think you should be gaining better results in examinations and tests. To help you do this we have asked senior staff and governors to work together more closely. This is to make sure the school is run better."

"Many of your teachers are working really hard to help you do well, but the things they try do not always help to improve exam results."

"Though the acting headteacher and his senior colleagues have done a great deal for the school, the school and... ...Local Authority are very much aware of the need to settle matters with regard to overall leadership of the school. Whereas in a big school each subject has a team of teachers with a 'head of department', this is a problem in a small school; things need to be done to make this aspect of management more effective."[82]

Such comments undermine student confidence in their teachers and breach the normal protocol of the learning environment. Teachers, in writing reports, address weakness or provide development points only for the individual concerned. They do not believe it appropriate to share criticism of one individual with another. Staff in schools which have been placed in Special Measures or given a Notice to Improve sometimes feel that such letters provide easy ammunition for students already disaffected, disillusioned and demoralised. Such letters do not contribute to the mandate for improvement but increase anxiety, undermine the students' pride in their school and threaten belief in themselves and what they can achieve. They may also provide additional encouragement to parents of students who are achieving well, to remove them and place them elsewhere, so increasing the proportion of vulnerable students in the school. For some students, such comments may

---

[82] Ofsted letters to pupils within Ofsted reports 2005-2007

constitute an explanatory style which enables students to excuse lack of effort. Mansell (2007) makes a similar point:

> "Hyper-accountability assumes, implicitly, that pupils have a right to high grades (or at least to perform as well as others have done, given their statistical starting points) and that if they have not received them, the failing is entirely their teachers'. So instead of pupils getting the message that their hard work will lead to success, and to take responsibility for their actions, they are given the signal that it is down to the teacher to deliver that achievement for them."[83]

Respect is widely recognized as a fundamental human need. Young people expect to be respected and respond well to adults who show regard for them and their views. Working with the young, especially with vulnerable students, is stressful and a pattern of lack of mutual respect between parents and their children often results in challenging behaviour in school. Staff working with students need to be accorded the same respect, not merely by their students but by those institutions and authorities who employ them. Schools are expected to promote respect and all those who are charged with supporting schools and helping to raise achievement must ensure that the principle is extended to the whole school community.

---

[83] Mansell Warwick (2007) Education by Numbers: The Tyranny of Testing. Politico's

INCLUSION

"The key is to make it inclusive and exciting for all."

"If they come with huge complex difficulties, even if they don't achieve their potential by Year 11, we would expect to make a difference – they will leave Year 11 happier, with more confidence - sport and drama can make a difference."

"Literacy and special needs factors figure in exclusions."

One of the challenges which face all those involved in schools is how to provide an education which is inclusive and at the same time recognises the uniqueness of every individual, with differences in academic ability, skills, talents and pace of learning. Once schools take into account differences of culture, ethnicity, social background, language, religion and the moral and spiritual needs of individual students, the challenge mounts. Given the constraints of buildings, funding, recruitment of staff, different levels of parental support and external support services' effectiveness, schools are faced with limited choices and hard decisions. This is made more difficult if external assessments, used to measure progress in certain aspects of education, are taken at specific points and their results used to compare one school with another.

> "Exclusion becomes a more attractive option, conformity to external priorities impedes attention to individuals and funding for schools with greater proportions of vulnerable young people becomes another constraining factor" (Reed and Hallgarten (2005))

In his speech to the DfES/Demos/OECD Conference in 2004[84], David Miliband argues that education must be 'shaped to individual need.' He sets out principles of personalised learning

---

[84] Miliband David (2004) Speech *'Choice and Voice'* to DfES/Demos/OECD Conference

with which few would disagree. However the conclusions drawn concerning the importance of parental choice and pupil voice do not sit well with the market imagery in which the speech is steeped. He calls for a more rigorous gifted and talented programme, but does not appear to recognise an arguably more pressing matter of personalisation for the disadvantaged and excluded. Searle (2001) would argue that "an inclusive school cannot exist if it accommodates itself within a system of market competition and rivalry"[85]

The introduction of the GCSE was designed to enable greater inclusion. It combined O-Levels and CSE examinations in order to achieve equal access and the emphasis was clearly on 'positive achievement' – the examination was established to reward what the candidate 'knows, understands and can do.' A*-G grades are therefore passes – only a U is a failure. Keith Joseph, Secretary of State for Education intended that 90% of candidates should achieve at least a grade F. The aim was to reward achievement on appropriate tasks at each level, rather than have levels of failure.

It is important in personalised learning that students are able to develop at their own optimum pace. If educational success is reduced to those academic skills which are most easily measured, in narrow fields of study, and measured at set points along the route, then it will cease to be inclusive. Tests at prescribed intervals reinforce failure – a student may fail to achieve a Level 4 at 11, fail to gain a Level 5 at 14 and fail to obtain a Grade C at GCSE. Multiply these results by the number of test, mock exams and practice questions they have undertaken and it is not hard to see that they are not likely to feel 'included'. The reinforcement of failure at each stage is underlined. If to this is added a public perception of failure as test results and league tables are published

---

[85] Searle Chris (2001) An Exclusive Education. Race, class and exclusion in British schools. Lawrence and Wishart

and discussed, it is not hard to understand why vulnerable students become disaffected or disengaged.

> "The sense of being a low priority to the teachers in the school comes across powerfully in the accounts of the young people in my sample... A key problem is that an academic market-orientated system may work against inclusive values." (Hilton (2006) p 308)[86]

The Institute of Fiscal Studies (Brewer et al. 2004)[87] showed that economic inequality in the UK had become the most important cause of social exclusion and child poverty (c.f. Thrupp, 2005; Boyle et al. 2006). The UNICEF report (2007) providing an overview on the lives and well being of children in 21 countries places the UK at the bottom of the average overall ranking position and second from the bottom for the percentage of children (0-17) in households with equivalent income of less than 50% of the median (UK 16.2% mean=11.2%) The pressures on the young have been noted and drugs and alcohol provide one sure path to 'inclusion' of a kind, with immediate acceptance into a sub-culture – such as are well documented in the press. According to the UNICEF survey (2007 p 29) 30.8% of young people in the UK reported being drunk on two or more occasions (mean=15.4%). 34.9% of UK children reported to have used cannabis in the last twelve months (mean=21.4), regular use of which is associated with depression, physical ill-health, problems at school and other forms of risk-taking. Cannabis may also trigger psychosis. 38.1% of young people in the UK had had sexual intercourse by the age of 15 – compared with the other sixteen countries with appropriate data – where the percentage is between 15% and 28% (mean=23.6).

---

[86] Hilton Zoe (2006) Disaffection and School exclusion: why are inclusion policies still not working in Scotland. *Research Papers in Education* 21 (3) 295-314

[87] Brewer M, Goodman A, Myak M, Shaw J, & Shepherd A (2004) Poverty and inequality in Britain. Institute of Fiscal Studies: London

Perhaps in view of these and other statistics, it is not surprising that the UK is close to the top of the teenage pregnancies table with approximately 28 births per 1000 women aged 15-19 (2003) (mean= 16). This may be significant in terms of the unhappiness which teenagers may experience and the perceived happiness which may result from a birth:

"To a young person with little sense of current well-being – unhappy and perhaps mistreated at home, miserable and under-achieving at school, and with only an unskilled and low-paid job to look forward to – having a baby to love and be loved by, with a small income from benefits and a home of her own, may seem a more attractive option than the alternatives."[88]

Government programmes continue to focus largely on contraception and its availability, but it may be that more effective strategies should involve lifting self-esteem, providing for inclusion, raising aspirations and ensuring a successful educational outcome for all. This cannot be done in a culture which appears to value academic excellence and material wealth as opposed to the happiness of each individual and their contribution to society.

Unfortunately for some, in the last years of compulsory education, the school seems an irrelevancy and an unnecessary daily reminder of failure. Davies and Lee (2006) summarise the situation well. "In the case of non-attenders, self-withdrawers – they offer a critique of the school and the system and solve their personal problems by refusing to engage."[89] Riley and Rustique Forrester (2002 p72) comment:

"We found that the problem of pupil disengagement with the curriculum surfaced particularly with the older pupils (years 10-11) who described feelings of pressure, despair, hopelessness and

---

[88] UNICEF Report Card 7 2007 Child Poverty in perspective- An overview of child well-being in rich countries
[89] Davies John Dwyfor and Lee John (2006) 'To attend or not to attend? Why some students choose school and others reject it.' *Support for Learning* 21 No 4

intimidation which they attributed to their impending examinations."[90]

The tragedy for some is that schools do not have the levels of staffing or the resources to cope with such deep-rooted disaffection and alienation. Some of these young people exhibit challenging and highly disruptive behaviour and all require much individual attention and opportunities for alternative and flexible learning arrangements. Permanent exclusions inevitably follow, often as angry and rejected young people become health and safety risks to others. This would seem to be supported by recent permanent exclusion figures for Oxfordshire. In 2005-2006, 57% of permanent exclusions were for persistent disruptive behaviour, (37%) or assault on adults or pupils (20%). In 2006-2007, 73% of permanent exclusions were accounted within the same categories, with 43% given for assault on adults or pupils.

Pressure to meet non-academic targets also disadvantages vulnerable young people. Schools, if acting from self-interest, have every reason to increase permanent exclusions considerably. As Mansell (2007)[91] points out, permanent exclusion improves league tables, assists inspections and helps to retain staff. It is certainly a response to the relentless pressure schools face. Searle (2005) confirms this effect on disadvantaged and vulnerable young people, as he notes that, since league tables for truancy rates and unauthorised absences were introduced in February 1993, between 1993 and 1995 many permanent exclusions followed. "By permanently excluding students, a school's figures could miraculously improve – expelling chronic truants became a way of 'tidying up' the truancy figures."[92]

---

[90] Riley K and Rustique Forrester (2002) Disaffected students. London, Paul Chapman p 72
[91] Mansell Warwick (2007), Education by Numbers: The Tyranny of Testing Politico's p 220
[92] Searle Chris (2001) An Exclusive Education. Race, class and exclusion in British schools. Lawrence and Wishart

"Many have argued that the climate of growing competition between schools, coupled with the national inspection system and the publication of league tables of school performance, appear to have contributed to a rise in pupil exclusions"[93]

Mansell (2007) gives an example of a secondary school prepared to stand by its most difficult and vulnerable students which then found itself in Special Measures. It could have permanently excluded students but this would have left them adrift, producing angry young people and unhappy families. Another school provided work experience and suitable work-related learning which was appropriate but did not have GCSE equivalence; this too found itself in difficulties. [94] Both schools were committed to keeping the young people on their roll and minimising further damage, but they paid a heavy price for inclusion.

Headteachers in the study believed that personalised and flexible curriculum arrangements, good teaching and appropriate challenge and reward were keys to success with most young people.
Numbers permanently excluded were small and headteachers did not believe that decisions to permanently exclude had been affected by statistical considerations. The exception to this had been in the year when a PSA target was being sought (worth £1m to the LA) and some had experienced Local Authority pressure to agree a transfer rather than to permanently exclude. This is supported by the figures which showed a 50% drop for 2004-2005 only. Generally headteachers wanted to avoid a permanent exclusion wherever possible, acknowledging a commitment to the young person to give them every opportunity to succeed. They recognised that in many cases, moving vulnerable young people with complex needs from one mainstream setting, where they had failed, to another was not beneficial and was not in the spirit of

---

[93] Riley K and Rustique Forrester (2002) Disaffected students. London, Paul Chapman p15
[94] Mansell Warwick (2007) Education by Numbers: The Tyranny of Testing Politico's p208

67

inclusion. They were also aware that having to take permanently excluded students from another school was a considerable challenge and provided at least as many, if not more, problems for the receiving school. Thus in collectively keeping the pool small, they were opting to deal with their own, as far as possible, rather than receive those who had 'failed' elsewhere.' However high levels of disaffection, anger, frustration, neglect together with learning and other special needs led to incidents where the health and safety of the young person themselves and of others left little choice. They did reluctantly exclude if they felt that the safety and well-being of others was at stake or, if a first or second permanent exclusion might give the student priority access to special provision which would meet their needs. One headteacher reported that within a period of three years, seven students had been permanently excluded, four of whom were then placed appropriately in special provision. In only one case had the parents appealed, the majority believing that the school had done all it could and the decision might hasten more appropriate provision.

If inclusion in education means opportunity to thrive in education provision appropriate for each individual, then the special centres which schools run, pupil referral units and special schools all have an important part to play. A report commissioned by David Cameron found that 146 special schools have been closed since 1997, with the loss of 9000 places.[95] Baroness Warnock, responsible for the report which urged for greater integration of students with special educational needs in mainstream settings, was reported to have said that the inclusive approach had gone too far. She 'believed the system was failing thousands of vulnerable youngsters.'[96] Headteachers in the study regarded special schools as playing a vital part in ensuring that all students were properly

---

[95] Interim Recommendations for Consultation by The Commission on Special Needs (2007) Chair Sir Robert Balchin reported by Daily Mail James Chapman *Pupils 'are being failed' by closure of special schools* 31.7.07
[96] Baroness Warnock Warnock U-Turn on Special Schools. reported in Daily Telegraph. 9.6.2005

included. The weakness of some national and local strategies which followed the Warnock Report lay in the failure to recognise that special schools were part of the 'inclusion' of all students in education.

Inclusion acknowledges that each individual may have special individual talents, skills, needs and preferences. It also recognises that there are many different ways of learning and that standard class sizes are not appropriate learning settings for all. Personalised learning was therefore an important feature of the schools represented by the headteachers. Creative curriculum development, personalised timetables, small group and individual work, opportunities for more vocational and practical courses, appropriate work and community experience, early entry for public examinations and off-site provision were all strategies used to assist inclusion.

An inclusive curriculum will be a flexible one, with pathways to suit individual needs and interests. As young people develop more quickly, fast-tracking is becoming a common feature in schools, and not only for gifted and able young people. If research about learning in the classroom recognises the importance of variety, challenge and active learning, then the same must be true of the curriculum as a whole. In many schools now, GCSEs are being awarded before the end of Year 11. Vulnerable students in particular have gained from this practice. A GCSE acquired at the end of Year 9 can provide much of the encouragement needed to proceed successfully with other courses. Self-esteem rises and the student experiences success at a relatively early stage of their secondary school career. They may discover that, perhaps for the first time in their lives, they are 'ahead of the game.'

A note of caution needs to be given about national or even county strategies for ensuring maximum inclusion and engagement, in which all can reach their potential. Connolly (2005), having studied the effects of social class and ethnicity on gender differences in GCSE attainment, warns:

> "A danger remains therefore, in an approach that attempts to construct educational programmes, even for particular groups of pupils such as 'white working-class boys', in the belief that schools across the country can then simply use them directly with their own pupils. Rather there is a need for educational initiatives that are tailored much more directly to the particular needs of pupils in specific classes and schools" [97]

This acknowledges the importance of each school finding solutions appropriate to their needs which take into account the requirements and resources of the local area (c.f. 1944 Education Act)

A strong school ethos is clearly an important factor in inclusion. Lindsay and Muijs[98] investigated whether, in order to raise boys' attainment, the targeting of particular groups was more or less effective than a more universal commitment to treating all groups equally. They found in fact that successful schools combined various strategies and success was specific to particular contexts. However, the positive and inclusive attitude of all staff, which emphasised and celebrated the importance of education for everyone was powerful. Schools need the same approach to be adopted by those at the level of both local and national government. It is more difficult for schools to celebrate the success of students who have, for example, gained 10 D grades across a wide range of subjects, achieving more than their predicted grades, if they are regarded nationally as 'failures'. Inclusion in the society to which they are about to contribute demands proper recognition of achievement.

---

[97] Connolly, Paul (2006) 'The effects of social class and ethnicity on gender differences in GCSE attainment; a secondary analysis of the Youth Cohort Study of England and Wales 1997-2001' *British Education Research Journal* Feb 32 (1) pp3-21

[98] Lindsay G University of Warwick, Muijs D.(2006) Challenging underachievement in boys *Educational Research* 48 No 3 pp 313-332

Inclusion is again a principle which if valid for all students, needs to be applied to all schools. If schools are to do their best work, each one must be seen to be fully included in the educational effort. The notion of failing schools, taking them over, or bussing students to other communities, excludes local communities and undermines the provision available to their children. There are many opportunities at present to enable such commitment to all schools to become a reality. If all schools are Specialist Schools, working within partnerships of schools on an equal basis, much can be achieved. A national commitment to all schools in their communities is required, with appropriate support to enable each to answer the needs of its community. An ethos of inclusion needs to begin with a commitment to all schools at the highest level.

EMPOWERMENT

CREATIVITY AND INSPIRATION

"Although (targets) have raised expectations, they have also made GCSE teaching slightly 'duller' –e.g. teaching to the exam."

"Personal Social and Health Education (PSHE) is sidelined somewhat –because there is no accreditation."

"Education is about more than exams. We are right to be concerned about how our children seem to be falling behind. But we are also right to insist that education is about something more. Ruskin College reminds us that education is about opening minds not just to knowledge but to insight, beauty, inspiration. Schools and colleges which are good academically are often also dedicated to helping every student develop as an individual. They create a community of learning that is about personal growth as well as personal achievement. Ruskin has since its inception provided top-class education for people with top-class minds but no qualifications, teaching them about others but also teaching them about themselves, and in the process helping them to change direction in their lives."[99] (Tony Blair MP 1996)

This prelude to more than ten years in which education has been almost entirely judged on examination results underlines the impact of an accountability framework on values and policy. Blair referred in 1996 to schools and colleges 'which are good academically' being dedicated to helping every student develop as an individual. All schools would see this as their role. It is interesting that a number of headteachers of independent schools, well-known for their academic success, have warned about the pitfalls of excessive testing and the desirability of ensuring that the whole child is not neglected. Tony Little, Headteacher of Eton College, has said, "We have got into a habit of assessing

---

[99] Tony Blair MP 1996 Ruskin College, Oxford.

everything that young people do." Some have been quite outspoken in relation to government policy as it stifles creativity and impedes the development of skills and talents.[100] Clarissa Farr, High Mistress of St Paul's Girls School commented:

> "'Under this Government, students are facing more and more exams. There should be as little time as possible spent testing and much more time firing the imaginations of young people."[101]

Learning is an exciting activity. In a school, all are learning and building further on prior learning. The aim of education, to develop 'lively enquiring minds', places the teacher in a privileged position. He or she has already been fired with enthusiasm for learning, sufficient to enable them to gain a degree and professional qualifications. Their greatest reward is to see their students inspired, producing creative work, making insightful contributions to a course, asking questions and developing their understanding of themselves and the world. Scientists such as Alec Jeffrey, who developed the DNA fingerprinting technique, and the Nobel Prize winner Professor Martin Evans have spoken of their childhood –their natural curiosity and their excitement as they reflected and experimented. Teachers have the opportunity to nurture such exploration and fire such enthusiasm.

If schools are to produce gifted scientists, teaching must provide all students with opportunities for creativity and experiment. Teachers need time to facilitate this kind of learning, at all levels and across all abilities. It cannot be surprising that at present, many students, particularly those whose literacy skills are not developed or who are disadvantaged in other ways, describe their lessons at school as dull and boring, following a well-worn and unengaging routine (Riley and Rustique Forrester, 2002). Schools are well aware that

---

[100] e.g. Martin Stephen, St Paul's School (Daily Mail 1.12.07), Anthony Seldon, Wellington School, John Witheridge, Charterhouse (D Telegraph 25.8.07) Tony Little, Headteacher of Eton College (D Telegraph 11.2.08)
[101] Clarissa Farr, St Paul's Girls School (D Telegraph 1.9.07)

part of the answer in addressing the needs of vulnerable young people lies in providing an inspiring and creative curriculum in which students want to be fully engaged. National policies currently dictate a different regime and fear of inspection stifles initiative. As Barton (2007) reports:

"Ofsted should be reminding us, time and again, what it is that great teachers do to lift the expectations and performance of their students to the next level. Instead, too often, it feels like an ongoing onslaught of criticism –what they don't see rather than what they do."[102]

Lovey (1999) indicates that while a Conservative government promised choice and diversity, its education policy led to more and more pupils becoming disaffected at an earlier age.

"The nature and demands of the National Curriculum and its associated testing arrangements appeared to be associated with increased problems of pupil disengagement. The matter was compounded as competition between schools widened the gap between those who were empowered by the choices they were offered and those for whom there was little or no choice. It also created sink schools as well as prosperous ones. In these situations, it was difficult for children to see education as the key to all doors."[103]

When Labour came to power in 1997, even more constraints were placed on schools and on students, and initiatives abounded. The Prime Minister's mantra 'education, education, education'[104] was intended to emphasise a commitment to make education a priority. Education was seen as a way of counteracting the effects of poverty and disadvantage and of producing a skilled and flexible

---

[102] Barton, Geoff (2007) Shouldn't Ofsted be helping us to improve our schools? National Education Trust p7
[103] Lovey Jane (1999) *Disengagement, Truancy and Exclusion in New Labour's Policies for Schools.* ed Docking J p194
[104] Tony Blair Labour Party Conference 1996

workforce. Unfortunately, under the guise of accountability, measurement of 'progress' has led to increased emphasis on testing, targets and league tables and stark judgments on what constitutes success and failure have narrowed the focus and increased the achievement gap. One study of the effect of the new policies on disaffected young people (Lovey et al., 1993) investigated excellent hands-on provision at a farm. It reported:

"The staff are frustrated at the prospect of a National Curriculum which, if followed exactly, would provide an unacceptable strait-jacket on what is now an exciting and innovative project which serves well a group of young people in one of the most notoriously deprived areas of the country"[105]

Many studies have recognised the damage being done to education by these policies. Brehony (2005) summarises the pressure which was coming to bear on the policies in place at the beginning of the Blair government. He reports that in 1999, the Director of the Think-Tank (Demos), Tom Bentley, argued that the emphasis on qualifications should be reduced and that creativity was important. He and others believed that 'test-mania' meant that young people's creativity had been 'squeezed out' of the curriculum (Jupp et al., 2001[106]) The tension between the over-management of teachers and their classroom practice and the need to encourage creativity and innovation had been recognised (Hartley, 2003).

The narrowing effect of the National Curriculum and the disadvantages of such prescription are widely recognised (Reay and Wiliam, 1999; Whitty et al, 1998; Perryman, 2007). Mansell

---

[105] Lovey, Jane., Docking Jim and Evans, Ray (1993) *Exclusion from School: provision for disaffection at KS4* David Fulton in assoc with the Roehampton Institute.
[106] Jupp R, Fairly C., Bentley, T., Demos and Design C (2001) *What learning needs: the challenge for a creative nation* London Demos/Design Council quoted in Brehony Primary schooling under New Labour: the irresolvable contraction of excellence and enjoyment. *Oxford Review of Education* 31 (1) 29-46

(2007) notes that particularly in Year 6, students now have less PE, Art, Music and slightly less History and Geography. Between Christmas and May, 44% of the total teaching time in Year 9 is taken up with preparation for the SATs. The National Curriculum is not seen to be pupil centred (Alexander, 2004; Brehony, 2005).

"The prescribed core of the National Curriculum... provides the motivation for wide-scale truancy, self-exclusion and under-achievement, as well as the disaffection and rebellion which can characterise much of their (pupils') school life" (Searle, 2001 P 85)

The rigidity of the National Curriculum is regarded as one of the factors leading to students' disaffection and non-attendance at school (Reid, 2006). Another study (Whitty et al., 1998) commented "We have seen in England and Wales in recent years the imposition by central government of a narrow and nationalistic National Curriculum, which seems to exclude minority ethnic and disadvantaged groups"[107]. The Bow Group (2007)[108] has highlighted the figure of 26,000 students as failing to achieve a single GCSE, blaming a 'relentless focus upon academic curriculum' and Mick Brookes, General Secretary of the NAHT, has referred to those leaving school with no or very few qualifications, given the disappearance of many unskilled jobs, as 'an army of the unemployable'.[109] Riley and Rustique Forrester (2002) conclude:

"Our findings suggest that for many children on the margins, school is a deeply boring experience which can also be hazardous and demeaning. By and large, this is not because teachers are uncommitted to the needs of disaffected children, but because both

---

[107] Whitty, Geoff, Power, Sally.,Halpin, David (1998) Devolution and Choice in Education: The School, the State and the Market. Open University Press P 139
[108] Skidmore, Chris; Cuff, Nick (2007) *'Wasted Education'* The Bow Group cited in www.publicfinance.co.uk in Feature 'Comment; Doing what works by Nick Cuff.
[109] Brookes Mick General Secretary NAHT Annual Conference 2007, reported in Daily Telegraph August 2007

teachers and pupils are locked into an educational system which gives them little room to manoevre."[110]

Searle (2001) in a study on exclusion also concludes that the National Curriculum is responsible for the boredom, underachievement and rebellion of many young people. He refers to the 1970s when teachers in inner cities were trusted with the curriculum and suggests that they would have been insulted to have been required to teach to a formula. They knew they had to be creative and respond to the local needs of the different communities a city school would serve.

"The constant threat of an impending Ofsted inspection is becoming a severe menace to adventure, audacity and experiment in teaching – and the kind of pedagogical risks teachers need to take to stimulate and provoke the imagination and motivation of their most unwilling students."[111]

Within the primary phase, Alexander (2004) argues that government promises of greater autonomy, greater emphasis on self-evaluation, creativity and pupil-centred learning are contradicted by "the continued pressure of testing, targets and performance tables and the creeping hegemonisation of the curriculum by the Literacy and Numeracy Strategies, with three-part lessons, interactive whole-class teaching and plenaries soon to become a template for the teaching of everything."[112]

Headteachers interviewed were aware of the constraints but keen to maintain a wide range of opportunities, making curriculum decisions relating to breadth and balance. They were not convinced

---

[110] Riley, Kathryn, Rustique-Forrester, E (2002) Working with disaffected students. London Paul Chapman p 97
[111] Searle Chris, (2001) An Exclusive Education: Race, class and exclusion in British schools. Lawrence Wishart
[112] Alexander Robin (2004) Still no pedagogy? Principle, pragmatism and compliance in primary education.
Cambridge Journal of Education 34 (1) 7-34

that the curriculum should be determined by arguments of economic utility or by levels in qualifications, but acknowledged that courses without accreditation or GCSE equivalence were more difficult to justify in the current climate.

The tensions caused by league tables published three times during the year[113] add to the pressures on schools, underline differences and can create anxiety throughout the year. Brehony (2005) notes the contradictions between ideological elements issuing in targeted interventions to address poverty and disadvantage, together with commitment to creativity and flexibility, set against the targets, testing and inspection policies which impede progress towards them. He writes, with reference to inspection in primary schools:

> "This situation might be acceptable if it could be shown that pupils were benefiting from their policies not just in terms of test results but also in respect of fairness and social justice. There is, unfortunately, little evidence that this is the case."[114]

The public, picking up on the language used to describe schools, have begun to distrust state schools in general – they all obviously need 'improving'. If teaching and learning is only 'satisfactory', this clearly isn't good enough and an 'inadequate' lesson must be a shambles. They remain largely unaware of the rigid criteria against which a lesson is being judged i.e. it must have objectives clearly stated, students should be actively engaged, lessons should not be too 'teacher-led', and there must be evidence of learning taking place i.e. a plenary in which students can show what they have learnt. While much of this is good practice, it may not be right or appropriate to teach every lesson in this way. Active learning does not always mean students 'doing' things. The brain can be active

---

[113] August, (GCSE A Level) January (GCSE A Level CVA) February (KS3)
[114] Brehony, Kevin J. (2005) Primary schooling under New Labour: the irresolvable contradiction of excellence and enjoyment. *Oxford Review of Education* 31(1) 29-46 p 42

even when the lesson is 'teacher-led'- much depends on the inspiration and creativity of the teacher and some young people thrive on this method of teaching.

It is interesting to consider whether those in grammar or independent schools in the nineteen sixties and seventies were provided with 'inadequate' lessons from start to finish? Yet many teachers inspired, influenced and motivated their students and saw them off to colleges and universities, into industries and professions. And while such students were largely higher achievers and the majority well-motivated, the point here is that 'one size does not fit all'. Good and outstanding teaching is recognised by students and educationalists alike but part of the professionalism of a good teacher is their ability to maximise learning and take advantage of opportunities as they present themselves. Formulaic methods of teaching, together with the constraints of curriculum delivery and assessment, have disempowered the profession. Teachers do not now feel in control of the curriculum or of teaching methods. They are expected to accept new ideas as 'truth'– for example the learning styles (visual, auditory and kinaesthetic) for which there is no scientific basis (Kratzig and Arbuthnott, 2006). They would be concerned about any diversion from the tight scheme of work or any failure to meet the lesson objectives students have copied into their exercise books (Perryman 2007).

Some vulnerable young people do not flourish in normal classrooms, become bored by the routine and turn to disruption. They fear making mistakes, they are concerned about academic bullying, they are embarrassed at their relatively poor reading age and their unstable relationships make group work in a large class difficult. They respond much better to individual or small group work. They may need considerable encouragement and reassurance to begin work, a system of rewards and above all a creative and flexible approach in which teachers are able to tailor learning to interests and moods over longer or shorter periods of time.

The quality of the teaching has always been a crucial factor in learning, but teaching, real teaching, has never been about 'delivery' – it has included inspiration, encouragement, questioning, playing to strengths, engaging in thought and reflection and above all an ability to be flexible. There is little room for inspiration in a prescriptive and punitive climate. 'Enterprise' education is one of the latest requirements for secondary schools. Teachers who choose to engage in enterprising learning take a risk.

New Labour has been committed to taking initiatives to counteract the effects of poverty and disadvantage, but the persistence in testing and punitive measures undermines this and runs contrary to creativity and individual expression. An examination-orientated and league-table-driven curriculum has stifled independent creative working, as universities are discovering. It has also driven out vulnerable young people who see little point in engaging post-16 in a system which has already effectively rejected them as failures.

Moreover, given that the quality of teaching and the attitude of teachers to individual students are of great importance, programmes which are designed to maximise individual strengths and enthusiasms of the teachers involved are also likely to be the most successful. This again would indicate a caution in micro-management or over-direction from government. As Davies et al. (2005) indicate "teachers' self-direction is socially desirable in that contracts for teachers cannot be fully specified and it is desirable for schools and teachers to be innovative in response to local conditions and change."[115]

Durant (2007) is clear that effective headteachers enable initiative and that staff are given opportunities to take ownership of projects

---

[115] Davies, Peter, Coates Gwen, Hammersley-Fletcher, Linda and Mangan, Jean (2005)When becoming a 50% school is success enough: a principal-agent analysis of subject leaders' target setting. *School Leadership and Management* 25(5) 493-511

and involve themselves in the development of the school, 'refining or discarding initiatives as they think best.' He argues that leadership cannot function at all if dictated from above. 'The central direction of educational practice through national strategies, to the extent that currently occurs in England, and in the way that it stifles home-grown innovation, is contrary to good leadership.[116]

At present there is a commitment to take the views of students into account and student voice has been seen to make a significant contribution to self-evaluation processes. David Miliband in a speech in 2004, states

> "Students are not merely educational shoppers in the market place: they are creators of their own educational experience and their voice can help shape provision".[117]

Currently, however, targets and league tables are more likely to impact on provision than student voice. If students find the study of modern languages difficult or unattractive, and A*-C percentages are lower than other subjects, the government will not be surprised that schools opt to offer subjects in which they may have greater success. The fact that all students may have an entitlement to study a language is forgotten in the desperate drive to raise percentages - and again education is sacrificed on the altar of accountability. In the same way, if all students who do not take 8 GCSEs will adversely affect a school's Contextual Value Added, some vulnerable students will be driven into taking more GCSEs than they would wish to do. Students will be encouraged to take GCSE instead of, or in addition to, Entry Level, because the points

---

[116] Durant Danny The role of UK Local Authorities to support school improvement. Paper presented at the British Educational Research Association Annual Conference, Institute of Education, University of London, 5-8 September 2007.
[117] Miliband, David (2004) *Choice and Voice in Personalised Learning* Speech at a DfES Innovation Unit/Demos/OECD Conference Personalising Education: The Future of Public Sector Reform. p6

are greater. Courses which might be more appropriate, useful and above all engaging, but which do not have GCSE A*-C equivalence will be dropped in favour of those that do.

Oxfordshire headteachers were committed to a wide range of activities which they believe enhanced the learning process. Some of the most memorable learning experiences on which adults can reflect for many years are visits, outdoor education and residential experiences. Young people look forward to these, sometimes with a certain amount of apprehension, and then almost routinely enjoy the experience. Teachers know that, despite the considerable organisation involved, efforts will be well rewarded in terms of the quality of education provided and the growth which will occur. Eyes will be opened, perspectives altered, ideas suggested, learning stimulated and lives changed. For many vulnerable young people, such visits are still more important because they will not be made with their families. Yet far from supported in the provision of these activities, schools find themselves increasingly hampered by excessive health and safety demands, and teachers are led to believe that if anything goes wrong, they may face legal action. It is to the credit of the teaching profession that, given such discouragement, so many are prepared to provide these experiences for young people and that headteachers so wholeheartedly support them. The profession's view of education involves a commitment to the development of the whole child, far exceeding the demands placed on it by targets and testing. Oxfordshire headteachers in fact noted an increase in extra-curricular activity, with 87% reporting an increase within the last ten years in extra-curricular activities offered in their schools. It would appear that the profession continues to provide, despite constraints, what it recognises will inspire and empower young people.

PARENT PARTNERSHIP

"Parents are generally supportive and want children to do well. However, dysfunctional families contribute to students' poor attendance."

"We are seeing more parents now who are dysfunctional and who do not see education as a priority."

Education has often been described as a three way partnership between the school, the parents and the student. Teachers know that in cases in which parents did not have a good experience at school themselves or where they are antagonistic towards staff, students are more difficult to motivate and more likely to present challenges to staff. Riley and Rustique Forrester (2002) include comments from students which reflect these kinds of difficulties. Thus establishing good relationships with parents as well as their children is seen as a priority in addressing the needs of all students, but especially those who are vulnerable. (Lindsay and Muijs, 2006) Establishing supportive partnerships is seen by headteachers as an integral part of the role of Special Needs Coordinators, year leaders and tutors and all those with pastoral responsibilities in schools.

The transfer from primary to secondary school is usually one of concern for parents and schools are keen to establish good relationships with them. The pattern of involvement in secondary schools differs from that in primary schools, largely owing to the need for parents to undertake more paid employment as children get older, and the desire on the part of young people for greater independence from parents. Home-School Agreements are at least an acknowledgement of the fundamental role which parents play in encouraging their children to value their education and empowering them to be successful. Yet the effectiveness of this document is only as good as the relationships developed, the trust which parents feel they can place in the school and the quality of communication which follows. However, school staff understand

84

their role in loco parentis and the partnership in parenting is likely to develop well beyond the limits of the documentation.

William Stewart, reporting on a speech by Ed Balls, Secretary of State for Children Young People and Families, summarised his view that many children were not getting the right support from parents. They were not encouraged to do well, did not eat properly and were not inspired to do exercise. "This all has an effect on their ability to learn. They are only in school 14% of the time on average. We have to look outside the school gate."[118] While recognising that these are factors which lead to disadvantage, schools also know that increasing numbers of single parent families, unemployment, redundancy, rising living costs, housing difficulties and lack of parenting skills all play their part in creating vulnerability. Of the 21 'rich countries' UNICEF considered in Report Card 7 (2007), the UK is the second highest in terms of young people (aged 11, 13 and 15) living in single-parent or step-families.[119] In a study by the World Health Organisation (2004), difficulties in communicating with parents are seen to rise significantly between 11 and 15 years of age[120] Parents often struggle to control teenage children and with the increase in technology available to them, young people are increasingly communicating with their peers and others in a secret world of which parents are almost wholly unaware.

However, there is no evidence to suggest that parents of students from 'deprived homes' are not interested in their children's progress at school (Riley and Docking 2004). This was supported by headteachers who believed that parents were generally committed to their children's education. The Keele Schools Survey summary (2004) showed that 97% of students agreed or strongly

---

[118] Times Educational Supplement William Stewart 7th September 2007 P 3
[119] UNICEF Report Card 7 2007 Child Poverty in perspective- An overview of child well-being in rich countries.
[120] World Health Organization (2004) Health Behaviour in School-aged Children: report from the 2001-2002 survey.

agreed that parents thought it was important to do well at school and approximately 95% agreed that their parents made it clear that they should behave well at school. Headteachers considered that this was also true with regard to students who had been or were likely to be permanently excluded. Some parents blamed the school, but many felt that the school had done what it could and were upset or angry at their child's apparent inability to behave appropriately. Some were also frustrated at the lack of support by other agencies, particularly when they felt their children were out of control and getting into trouble. Difficulties with the police, young people staying out all night, fears of the effects of drugs and alcohol and of pregnancy were common concerns expressed by parents of vulnerable students.

Good communications with parents in relation to expectations and aspirations for all students was regarded as a key requirement for success. Thus work in a partnership approach with parents to support a vulnerable student is seen to be crucial if the young person is to benefit from a consistent message and a belief in their potential for success. The emphasis on sharing individual targets, particularly GCSE targets, with parents and students was seen by headteachers to be largely beneficial. It provided a sense of realism and a baseline from which meaningful discussion could proceed.

This practice was thought to be of great importance with parents of vulnerable students. Some capable of good academic achievement needed praising at home as well as at school. For some parents, the sharing of information proved more difficult, especially when parents were led to believe that 'C' was the minimum requirement for any future success. As a parent remarked "Ds and Es are no good to him. Are you saying he is too stupid to pass these exams?" Schools continue to emphasise different levels of GCSE pass, the acquisition of points, and the many opportunities available to students who achieve D-G grades. However such messages to parents are confusing as politicians and other public figures reported in the press consistently refer to D-G grades as 'fail' grades. These mixed messages place additional pressure on young people, set up unrealistic expectations, undermine the professional advice and guidance teachers are providing, and sometimes increase alienation from school and misery at home.

There is evidence that current policies relating to testing and league tables are additionally creating a different kind of vulnerable student as accreditation seems to equate to value. Parents who can afford it, engage private tutors to improve their children's chances of examination or test success. They introduce their children to activities in which they are pressed to achieve specific accredited standards. Independent schools no less than maintained schools notice this kind of behaviour on the part of some parents. While parents can provide important support for their children's education and their desire to offer them new activities is to be applauded, Vicky Tuck, Principal of Cheltenham Ladies College said "Parents need to be careful about getting the balance right between encouraging them to develop their interests....but also conveying to children they are loved for who they are rather than from having a set of medals, accolades or certificates."[121] Schools are seeing a new kind of anxiety from those who are not disadvantaged in the normal sense of the word, but are suffering from too great a pressure to achieve high levels or grades in examinations. The OECD study[122] found a link between pushy parents and underperformance. Nearly 40% of headteachers in Britain said there was 'constant' pressure on pupils to do well. The lowest rate was found in Finland, the best performing country.

Pressures to succeed at school are only part of a complex set of factors affecting the happiness of the student and the quality of family relationships. Some young people stay at home, afraid to leave their parents, required to run errands and look after children,

---

[121] Daily Mail 7th Nov, 2007
[122] OECD (2007) Education at a glance.

fearful of school society. According to the Bow Group[123], 15,000 students have disappeared from school rolls. Children are moved from one parent to another, families move suddenly for many different reasons, some are sent abroad for an extended holiday; young people are lost to the system, never to resume their education. Ofsted notes a clear relationship between deprivation, poor health and lower rates of attendance.[124] Vulnerable students with attendance problems include school refusers, those who are or believe they are being victimised or bullied, the disaffected and dysfunctional, those affected by drugs or night-time anti-social behaviour. Educational factors include poor reading ability, dislike of specific teachers or lessons and belief that the National Curriculum is a waste of time (Social Inclusion Unit, 1998; Audit Commission, 1996). Lovey (2000) adds a further factor - pressures on schools to meet performance targets. Their needs include individual tracking and attention, personalised programmes, careers advice, hope for the future and a taste of success. Teaching and support staff in schools take time to make relationships with parents and negotiate individual timetables which will facilitate better attendance and enable more parental support (Reid, 2006).

Equally, as part of the parenting support, headteachers expected to enlist additional support or mentoring from staff, and to involve agencies, health and social workers, home school links workers, police liaison officers, youth offending teams and others. 84% of the headteachers, since workforce remodelling, had appointed non-teaching staff to positions such as student welfare managers, or assistant heads of year. In one further case, the post was planned and awaiting the availability of funds to finance it. There was a widespread recognition of the need for such support as part of an educational process.

---

[123] Skidmore, Chris; Cuff, Nick '*Wasted Education*' The Bow Group cited in www.publicfinance.co.uk in Feature 'Comment; Doing what works by Nick Cuff.
[124] Ofsted *Her Majesty's Inspector's Annual Report* 2006-2007 p66

"I see it as my responsibility to engage and support parents who are losing it with their children. They need to be enabled to re-establish control if they can. We now have an army of support staff who fulfil this role." (Headteacher)

Headteachers expected to improve the attendance of some young people by providing good quality teaching, a creative and flexible curriculum and opportunities for personalised learning. Some remarked on noticeably improved attendance by individuals on their day at an FE college, or when participating in a vocational course. Sometimes such a change in environment and the prospect of success had a marked effect on attendance and behaviour back at school. Students were praised for their work, parents began to believe that their son or daughter could be successful and the relationship between school and home improved.

However, while the schools model good practice in supporting learning, based on research and their common ground with parents, central policy acts to counter such strategies. In order to ensure parents cooperate in the education of their children, legislation, threats and punishments are used to bring them into line. Punitive measures are advocated - for example, fining for non-attendance or for attendance when excluded, and in rare cases, imprisonment. Nor is it clear that such measures are effective. Ofsted has noted in relation to legal action to address attendance issues, "While these legal sanctions sent an important message to the pupils and their parents, and acted as a useful deterrent, their effect on the most disengaged pupils was limited."[125] The tone of the model formal fixed-term exclusion letter is also harsh 'Failure to attend a reintegration interview will be a factor taken into account by a magistrates court if, on future application, they consider whether to impose a parenting order on you.' Such practices are also in danger of setting up or increasing antagonism between school and the parents. This is not likely to improve the effectiveness of support for the young person.

---

[125] Ofsted *Her Majesty's Inspector's Annual Report* 2006-2007 P 71

Nor are schools exempt from this kind of punitive approach, which drives a wedge between parents and their children's school. Within the Education and Inspection Act 2006, there are new powers to investigate complaints about schools by parents, in which schools could be required to distribute widely to parents the judgment made in any given case. The potential for harm here is clear. While the existence of an external complaints procedure is important in a democracy, the enforced publicity of an individual grievance is unlikely to be productive. It is hard to conceive of a justification for yet another method of undermining parents' confidence in their school.

Governors in Disciplinary meetings and Appeals Panel members, meeting to rule on headteacher recommendations concerning exclusion, have found themselves having to conduct an adversarial-type meeting, when in reality the school has been working closely with parents for many months, supporting a vulnerable student. Where a case conference-style meeting would be more appropriate, legislation currently appears to advocate an adversarial approach. Frequently the parents and the school do not feel they are on different sides. Some parents of course believe an injustice has been done and wish to state their case. Many however acknowledge that much work has been done for the young person, understand why such a decision has been made and are desperate to know where to turn. Schools are placed in a difficult situation. Often the parents have other children in the school and the school does not wish to damage the partnership with parents. As staff act during the day in loco parentis, a system which divides those who have parenting responsibilities creates confusion in the minds of young people and destroys trust and stability. As the Ofsted report of 2006-7 comments:

"Anything which sets up school against parents is counterproductive and likely to have limited effect on vulnerable students"[126]

[126] Ofsted *Her Majesty's Inspector's Annual Report* 2006-2007 p71

While the government seems to believe that in a market economy the parent 'consumers' will create demand and drive supply, this model works for a minority, often those who are the most mobile. In reality most parents are not shaping education and, with current prescription, have never been further from doing so. Parents are generally happy with their children's schools - in 2004, 77% believed the school to be good or better [127] - chiefly because they are aware that the schools are providing for their children, a curriculum, both timetabled and hidden, based on a wider definition of education than the government appears to recognise or value, and that they are making good progress.

However, the recognition that education is more important than examination results and is fundamental to the welfare and future happiness of individuals and of the society in which they live and work seems to continue to be disregarded. As Thrupp and Tomlinson remark:

> "Evidence that the majority of parents prefer a good local school with a broad education, regardless of presumed abilities and aptitudes, at least to 16, is ignored."[128]

---

[127] Keele University (2004) Yearly average of the Schools Survey
[128] Thrupp Martin, Tomlinson, Sally (2005) Introduction: education policy, social justice and 'complex hope' *British Educational Research Journal* 31 pp549-556

A SENSE OF COMMUNITY

"The school lies at the heart of the community."

"There is a need for funding for greater in-school provision for vulnerable students."

A strong partnership of a school with its local community enables it to function most effectively. The community has much expertise and can offer support, advice and resources. This relationship is particularly valuable for vulnerable young people who can benefit from local expertise delivered within specific courses of study together with individual support through work experience, work shadowing, mentoring, or sponsorship. Companies may provide opportunities for visits, special consideration for a vulnerable student, key skills enhancement in an adult context and much more (Searle, 2001). Over years the school also builds up a reputation with the community for listening to parents and employers, supporting young people and providing advice and expertise.

One of the main aims of education must be to draw out potential from an individual to prepare him or her for a full life in a community. Not all young people are able to achieve equally in academic examinations; not all are talented in one specific area; not all perform equally across a range of basic life skills. Yet all are citizens, most will have paid employment and many will be parents and carers. A sense of community is therefore crucial for learning. Students see adults working together for common goals. They understand the need for rules, for justice and equality. They become understandably angry at injustice and victimisation. In schools where police liaison officers work, young people have opportunities to see them at work and at times some take part in restorative justice programmes. Vulnerable young people may build up relationships with community police officers, church and youth workers, Connexions staff or home-school links workers, who provide a different perspective, and schools facilitate the development of these relationships often to the benefit of families as well as students.

Vulnerable young people, who may not have good role models at home, who may be suspicious of help or kindness and who have not experienced love, stability or consistency, need time and attention which schools will try to provide. A school acts as a microcosm of society, a community in its own right. Within the schools, staff –and older students- become role models of good parents and good citizens. In a study of how effective schools raise boys' attainment, Lindsay and Muijs (2006) describe the 'school as community' as a key element in the success of the school in this regard. The study notes that in developing the partnership with parents, male parents and carers were being used in curricular and extra-curricular settings. "The involvement of male parents or carers in the academic achievement of boys in the schools really mattered."[129]   Another feature of recent support for vulnerable young people has been the appointment of young male teaching assistants, sometimes taking a gap year, who can have different kinds of conversations and can establish good relationships. Two Oxfordshire headteachers spoke warmly of the difference the appointment to the staff of such young people was making to some individual students.

The school is indeed a 'Second Home' and staff act in loco parentis. As locality working becomes a reality, it is hoped that young people and their families, and particularly those who are vulnerable, will receive more quickly and effectively the help they need. It would appear, from the value currently placed on targets, testing and league tables that the traditional parenting role of the school within its community has been underestimated, undervalued and forgotten. It is clear that evidence of its effectiveness in this area often lies in anecdotes, individual success stories and its

---

[129] Lindsay G, Muijs D., (2006). Challenging underachievement in boys. *Educational Research* 48 (3) pp 313-332

reputation for care within the families it serves. It also rests in prevention, statistics of which are not easy to obtain. However there is now much research to support this view. Such an immeasurable contribution to the life of the community does not sit well with a market-driven vision. Parsons (1999) underlines this point:

> "Schools are less than ever a community resource responding to a local, collective, democratic will. Their response to a national will has been enforced through curriculum stipulation, assessment and inspection which have focused on separate attainment within individualised 'marketised' schools"[130]

The punitive approach of present policies in closing or threatening to close 'failing' schools is unlikely to improve the lot of young people or the ability of parents to support their children. Gordon Brown has proposed closing 'failing' schools with fewer than 30% 5A*-C GCSE with English and maths.[131] Trevor Phillips, chair of the Equality and Human Rights Commission, suggested, following American practice, that there should be a limit on middle class children in 'good' schools or that students should be bussed to 'good' schools.[132] Such drastic proposals spring from a fundamental misunderstanding of the nature of education in community. These are knee-jerk responses to the understandable public reaction to the effects of government policies which include the production of league tables and the labelling of schools. In a study to discover whether market forces close the social and achievement gap, Merrett (2006) concludes:

> "Closing low SES[133] schools and moving their students to higher SES schools has therefore usually had a negative impact on the

---

[130] Parsons Carl (1999) Education, Exclusion and Citizenship. Routledge
[131] Daily Telegraph Brown threat to close one in five schools unless results improve. 1.11.07
[132] Daily Telegraph Equality chief wants limit on middle classes in top schools. 27.11.07
[133] SES=socio-economic status

achievement and the attendance of the receiving school and has not improve students' attainment overall"[134]

If there were greater support for each local school, greater funding for areas in most need and acceptance of difference and variation in academic results, all schools could be 'good' and parents would be happy to send their children to the local school, knowing that they would reach their potential. This is not to suggest that there would be no choice, but parents would be choosing between good schools, all offering strengths to the community.

Economic insecurity affects people of all skills levels and results in disruption and vulnerability to workers and their families. Living in poverty "leads to low self-esteem, eroded belief in what they can achieve and thus low expectations and withered motivation to learn." (Ranson, 1997)[135] Thrupp and Tomlinson (2005) in arguing for a fairer distribution of resources and a re-examination of market policies in education, make the point that much is left to be done to achieve a greater measure of social justice:

> "The creation of a competitive market state in which there is no level playing field for the disadvantaged to take part, is not socially just."[136]

Gilbert, Her Majesty's Chief Inspector, states in the 2006-2007 Annual Report:

---

[134] Merrett G (2006) Higher standards, better schools for all - a critique; can market forces close the social and achievement gap? *Improving schools* 2006 9 (93) p95 Sage publications

[135] Ranson Stewart, (1997) For citizenship and the remaking of civil society. in Affirming the Comprehensive Ideal Ed. R Pring and G Walford London, Palmer

[136] Thrupp Martin, Tomlinson Sally 2005 Introduction: education policy, social justice and 'complex hope' *British Educational Research Journal* 31 (5) Oct 2005 pp549-556

"The relationship between poverty and outcomes for young people is stark; the poor performance of many children and young people living in the most disadvantaged areas is seen in the Foundation Stage Early Learning Goals, in National Curriculum test results, and in GCSE results. Participation in higher education continues to have much to do with socio-economic background.........With good schools and support services around them, children find their disadvantage reduced..."[137]

Within the Ofsted report a chapter on 'Improving life chances: narrowing the gap' refers to the growing gap in the achievement of looked after children – 12% gaining 5A*-C and 63% gaining at least one GCSE. (National statistics are 59% and 98% respectively) Here again the needs of another very vulnerable group of young people are not being met. Schools make provision for them, but if their needs are great, as they may well be, then scarce resources which could assist small group provision and individual 'catch-up' tutorials etc is having to be diverted to ensure a school's survival in the 5A*-C contest. There is no direct additional funding available for schools which enables such vital individual intervention for students in the looked after system.

Parsons (2005) refers to the Ofsted 1996 Report comment on 12,000 permanent exclusions: "No democracy can afford to write off thousands of its young people." and comments "they are wrong!" He includes statements by other commentators referring to an unfair society, one in which state care of young people is inadequate, delinquents are locked up and young people commit suicide while in prison. Education can be a means of preventing harm, promoting stability and growth, opening doors, raising self esteem, but Parsons concludes:

---

[137] Gilbert, Christine (2006-7) *The Annual Report of Her Majesty's Chief Inspector* p6

"If those working in the field of prevention cannot, or do not fight on the political front, they collude in sustaining the current punitive approach." [138]

It is possible that locality working may facilitate a new approach to special provision, especially for those with great emotional and behavioural needs. If schools are empowered to act effectively as second homes, they may require discrete accommodation on a small scale, enabling young people who cannot cope in mainstream classrooms to experience a consistency of care and the opportunity to make progress at their own pace. Many schools have begun to provide such facilities but they are situated in limited accommodation and hampered by inadequate funding which restricts staffing and which cannot provide a full range of opportunities. Nevertheless headteachers reported many remarkable examples of individual success, given this kind of care and attention, even on a part-time basis.

If children are sent to the local school, a community school which serves the needs of the area, parents and children have many advantages. As they get older children can walk to school, child care is made easier, students can stay to enjoy after school clubs or activities more easily and with greater flexibility. Their friends are likely to live locally. Keeping in touch with school is easier and parents can 'pop in' - a small point, but one which alleviates anxiety for students and increases confidence. For some students, just knowing their parents live close by is reassuring. If funding were more equal and all schools were talked up nationally and in their localities, every school would be seen to be good, making a considerable contribution to the life and work of the community and its future.

---

[138] Parsons Carl (2005) School Exclusion: The will to punish. *British Journal of Educational Studies* 53(2) pp 187-211 p208

If parents are reassured that their local school is a good school, fewer children will leave friends behind and all will share in the success of a community school. It is clear that many schools going into Special Measures or becoming 'schools of concern' are successful in relation to many of the Every Child Matters outcomes and are working well with the community. Every school can therefore continue to identify its strengths and weaknesses and should be given appropriate support. Yet its presence in the community will be assured and the good it currently does will be celebrated. The community has a right to stability and an affirmation of educational values. Vulnerable young people and their families will benefit the most from this approach.

Collaboration is important and can produce considerable benefits to individual young people and to schools, but it will not be effective if collaboration is seen to be 'good' schools linking up with 'weaker' ones. Recognition of different degrees of challenge faced by different schools in a partnership is on the other hand essential. All schools are likely to have areas of good practice – departments which are doing well, systems which benefit children, individuals who are innovative and are making a difference. All schools and communities are entitled to believe that they can work on these and develop their own good practice. The Extended Schools initiative has similar potential for local communities, especially in providing further opportunities for vulnerable students. However once again, funding is inadequate and emphasis on sustainability often means that it is vulnerable students that fail to benefit.

When Specialist schools were first announced, the partnerships they were developing within their local community, and the contribution which they would make, was an important part of each bid, and funding had to be allocated from the school's grant specifically for these purposes. As the profile of standards and 'good' academic results has risen to be the overriding priority, so this part of a school's responsibility must be re-emphasised. One of the more exciting developments concerning the introduction of 14-19 Diploma courses is the opportunity this should present for schools to work more closely with the community. In turn, this should provide more opportunities for young people to find courses which suit their interests and talents, and for more employers and employees to be actively involved with young people. Schools are right to be concerned that the diploma content is not so academic that less able students or students who have specific learning difficulties cannot access such programmes or be inspired by them.

The failure of the system to make adequate provision for its young people most at risk is clear and the negative effect of current policies which pressurise schools into placing resources where they will most affect their standing in leagues tables is well documented (Mansell 2007). The closure of special schools and reduction in special school places by local authorities has placed more vulnerable young people in situations where there are not the resources to provide the education which meet their needs. If education is to contribute to good citizenship and a sense of community in which all may see their role, all schools need to be empowered to take initiative, to strengthen links with the community, to engage with role models. The task of the education of young people is a shared responsibility and privilege in which schools are actively involved with parents, peer groups, the media, employers and communities. Schools cannot afford to be deflected from this task by undue emphasis on one part of one outcome. If this cannot be achieved, poor and vulnerable young people are left to their own devices, alienated from a positive experience of learning and the taste of success. It is clear that where schools are able to engage with individual vulnerable young people, progress is made.

The school, a place of learning, is a fundamental symbol of democracy in a community. It is a place of trust - a place in which all expect to get a proper hearing and fair treatment. Care is provided and friendships and cooperation within the wider

community promoted. Parents normally regard a school as a place of reason. They know they will be heard; they expect an ethos of equal opportunities, justice, order and care. They are therefore at their most vocal if they believe the school has fallen short of the expected high standards. Parents and their children expect systems to be in place to enable young people to stand up for their rights, to fight injustice, to protect the weak and support good causes. They expect a place of learning to uphold reason and to empower their children with knowledge, understanding and skills to live an active life in a democratic community.

CONCLUSION

"I wonder when we will stand up and shout about the issue of targets, public league tables and inclusion."

"Despite the ridiculous pressure from the government... I remain very optimistic about our ability at grass roots level to make a difference"

Expectations

For vulnerable young people, government policies on targets, testing and league tables have been a tragedy. All students in the UK experience eleven years of compulsory education once in their lifetime. Most enter secondary school with high expectations and a desire for success. If they are not engaged in learning by 16, they may never be. There is a generation of young people growing up who have suffered while at school from an undue emphasis on that intellectual and academic achievement which can be accredited by public examinations, to the detriment of many other valuable assets which education can develop, enrich or facilitate. Many have attended schools which have suddenly been labelled as failing and many have left secondary education with low self-esteem and lower expectations.

Education is intended by definition to be learner-centred, but recent policy accords the learner little consideration. Significant questions need to be asked about the current micro-management and hyper-accountability which inevitably direct the work of schools. Has a belief in the uniqueness and value of every human being and their potential to contribute to the happiness of society given way to a uniformity of delivery and production designed simply to provide useful employees in the market place? Searle (2001) indicates that educationalists should promote "Values of generosity, community, solidarity, loyalty, cooperation, determination to gain a just and fulfilling education for all and the will to resist the meanness and selfishness of the market system"[139]

From the adoption of a market model, targets have followed, both for individuals and for institutions. Other public services such as the Health service and the Police are questioning the effects of targets on their work; many would see them causing as many difficulties as they solve, moving the challenges around rather than improving the service. There seems to be a widespread belief, by those making policy, that targets motivate people. Truly, goals are motivational, for all need to know the direction of travel. Yet over-ambitious targets, which may have essential funding resting on their achievement, 'forced' on individuals and schools, create anxiety, stress and sometimes alienation – an inherent dissatisfaction with the work and the potential for rejection. Targets manufacture a possibility for failure where none previously existed. In the inspection framework as published in September 2007, 'whether learners achieve their targets and whether the targets are adequately challenging' is part of the evaluation schedule for achievements and standards. If target-setting raises expectations on the part of the individual learner, it may motivate and engage. If it is seen as a stick with which to beat the learner into an acknowledgement of current under-achievement and lack of effort, it may alienate and lead to anxiety and disaffection. Sometimes targets have become labels on persons rather than performances, for example, 'I'm a G'. And so it is with schools. Targets set against achievement, used as weapons to designate individuals as 'failures' or schools as 'failing' may do untold damage to the lives of vulnerable young people, and add to their numbers. The Fischer Family Trust itself, faced with growing concern from schools under pressure from Local Authorities and

---

[139] Searle Chris (2001) An Exclusive Education: Race, class and exclusion in British schools. Lawrence and Wishart p140

Government, are now keen to emphasise that the figures it produces are 'estimates' not targets.

The progress and development of individual learners and the success of their schools cannot be judged merely on academic test and examination results. The current KS2 and KS3 tests contribute little to knowledge of a learner's educational progress or of the quality of the education learners are receiving. Many are asking the question, 'Who does testing at KS2 and KS3 benefit?'. Not the learners - they can be assessed at any time by professional staff with assessment moderated as required. Not the schools – their curriculum is constrained by preparation of and teaching to the tests, while staff know the level at which the students are working. Not the parents – they receive reports on progress regularly and watch anxious and sometimes demoralised young people show concern about their future and the imminent possibility of failure. The conclusion drawn here is that it is thought to benefit statisticians who are able to calculate 'progress' from baselines and politicians who want to run education as a business and not as a service to the community. In fact however, it widens the achievement gap, impedes a broad and balanced curriculum and undermines personalised learning. Arguably it fills the streets with aimless and disillusioned young people, whose only experience of success is their ability to lead or join supporting sub-cultures and harness the anger and fear of the society around them. Following a review of research in these areas of concern, Whitty et al. (1998, p126) concludes, "There seems little doubt that a combination of policies is enhancing the advantages of the already advantaged at the expense of the least well off."

Not all young people have the same academic ability. This statement needs emphasising because it seems to have been forgotten. Yet cognitive abilities tests show these differences and GCSE and A Level examinations are set to differentiate across the ability range. The very nature of an average means that a significant proportion will always be classed as 'below average'.

Given the range of cognitive abilities in a population and the wide variety of childhood experiences, one cannot expect every child to develop at the same rate or in the same ways. Some vulnerable students and some who are well adjusted, will not be able to achieve a C in the current maths specifications, even given many hours of good teaching each week. Their failure to grasp algebra or geometry does not mean they are destined to be poor citizens, parents or employees. The current spotlight on maths (English providing the higher percentages of C grades nationally) ensures that even more young people are in danger of being branded as 'failures'.

Gorard (2005) indicates that, in the same way as raw score values have been rejected as unrelated to school performance, value-added scores have to be rejected on the same grounds. The correlation between the two is 0.96. Following analysis of the difficulties inherent in league tables, and value-added techniques, he concludes "The enormity of the problem, once accepted, for policy making, the local reputations of schools and for students of school effectiveness would be difficult to over-emphasise."[140] He argues that families have been misled about the relative effectiveness of local schools, "with the schools in poorer areas, with academically weaker intakes, suffering the most from this misguided comparison dressed up as a 'fair test.'"[141]

The emphasis on 'Standards', and by this is meant a judgment on a narrow range of criteria from only a part of the whole secondary curriculum, damages the chances of vulnerable children. Such pressure on individual teachers promotes staff instability and discourages retention. It forces schools into categories and leads, especially in more challenging areas, to difficulties in recruitment. Headteachers' careers are placed on the line every three years and

[140] Gorard S (2005) *Value-added is of little value.* Paper presented at Br Educational Research Association Annual Conference Glamorgan p1
[141] Gorard S (2005) *Value-added is of little value.* Paper presented at Br Educational Research Association Annual Conference Glamorgan p7

further promotion for other staff is seen to be at risk simply because of their choice of school. Vulnerable students in disadvantaged schools are therefore further penalised as many talented and dedicated teachers fear to teach in a school which might be rejected as 'failing'. Progress will be slower as more time is spent on nurture, confidence building, and improving reading skills. Prior attainment has less significance from year to year than students' background and life experiences. Headteachers, primary and secondary, speak of the anxieties of the situation – "If I survive this Ofsted, I will move to an easier school." The pressure is now on them and their senior leadership teams. However well they may lead the school, however well their teachers may perform, if the young people cannot, for a multiplicity of reasons, produce the 'standards' and 'the value-added scores', then judgments will be 'satisfactory' at best. At worst, Special Measures and Notice to Improve categories will results in months and years of intervention, pressure, teaching to formula and test, more paperwork and great unhappiness. Resignations inevitably follow and instability and difficulties in recruitment increase.

The capacity to improve (a factor which is taken for granted in learners) is questioned in relation to schools. Yet teachers are, as a profession, self-critical and routinely seeking to develop their teaching in order that learners are better served. Learners in schools do not suffer complacent teachers gladly and the profession has supported the process of annual professional review. Yet capacity to improve is undermined either if schools are denigrated by ill-informed media comment or local politicians' rhetoric or if they are treated punitively when test results dip. No one should be surprised if, in these circumstances, puzzled and concerned parents choose to send their children elsewhere. A fall in roll leads to financial difficulties and increases in class-size - and vulnerable young people suffer further. Unfortunately it would appear that capacity to improve is compromised by the very policies at the heart of present accountability. If a school is labelled as 'failing', if young people are seen and see themselves as 'failures', if league tables are regarded as accurate and comprehensive statements about the quality of education provided by a school, then capacity for improvement is severely impaired and vulnerable young people are even more greatly disadvantaged.

Since the introduction of league tables in 1992, there has been a wealth of research in relation to testing, targets, league tables and inspections. Such research appears to have been largely ignored. The increasing tendency on the part of government to relate the management of education to a market economy and to regard parents as the consumers has been noted. Alongside this, there has been a growing concern of the numbers of students alienated from education and the social consequences for them and others that result from this phenomenon. Hilton comments that "schools became increasingly pre-occupied with publishable standards and grew to neglect the needs of lower ability groups who were unlikely to contribute to performance targets." Headteachers are aware that despite their best endeavours, the present system is weighted against attention being given to those unlikely to contribute to 5A*-C or even to the 5A*-G percentages. They know how important it is that vulnerable students are not neglected and marginalised. They direct resources to address their needs, but know that the results of these efforts will not gain widespread recognition. Those with higher examination results and a small proportion of vulnerable students can afford to make appropriate provision for them, irrespective of their inability to contribute to the statistical success of the school. Those serving more disadvantaged communities, where vulnerable young people form a significant proportion of the roll cannot afford to do the same.

"When the accountability stakes are high and schools are judged in terms of their examination performance and success in Ofsted inspections, broader social or educational goals tend to be put on the back burner, and children on the margins are seen as obstacles to the advance of national goals"[142]

And yet, despite all of this, 88% of children say they are happy at school[143] – a testimony to the dedication of staff in schools to their profession, which has enabled many of them to continue to provide for the young people, in addition to good teaching, all those things which cannot be measured, or are regarded currently as peripheral. All young people have a right to expect their lives to be enriched by learning, to experience achievement and taste success. Vulnerable students need all that schools can provide to take a full part in what is offered. They and their parents need to know that they are engaged in an education which promotes confidence in their abilities and above all their happiness.

Encouragement

Education has recognised for many years the importance of encouragement and praise. Motivation for learning increases with self-esteem. Confidence based on success in one area of learning can provide an incentive to try other areas. The apparent resilience of some vulnerable young people, in the face of relentless misery at home or shocking childhood experiences, can only be admired. Yet many hide their feelings and arrive in school fearful and demoralised, suspicious of adults, expecting injustice and bullying and convinced that the school will provide another opportunity for the imprisonment of body and spirit which will label them useless and worthless.

Every individual is entitled to believe that they count, that they are valued for what they are and what they are able to offer. They have a right to an education which will encourage them to find themselves and build on their strengths, which will praise their

---

[142] Guardian (7.3. 2000) – cited by Riley K, Rustique Forrester (2002) Working with Disaffected students. London Paul Chapmanp14.
[143] Keele University (2004) Yearly average of the Schools Survey

achievements and acknowledge their success. Throughout their education, students are introduced to new experiences in which their talents can be displayed. If lack of effort masks fear of failure, then encouragement to achieve is vital. Young people crave respect and disaffected students will not accept humiliation.

If personalised learning is to mean what it says, then each child cannot be expected to arrive at the same point at the same time. Key Stage 2 and 3 tests stand in the way of progress - they waste almost a year for many children – and their outcomes only show that most children can pass a test for which they are given mock papers, booster classes, revision sessions and drilling on mark schemes for months on end. Importantly they are providing many vulnerable young people with early experience of repeated failure and dull routine and creating vulnerability where none previously existed.

> "Lower-achieving students are doubly disadvantaged by summative assessment since being labelled as failures has an impact not just on current feelings about their ability to learn, but lowers further their already low self-esteem and reduces future effort and success".[144]

While it is likely that most young people will be, and will want to be, engaged in education or training until they are eighteen, it may not be appropriate for all – especially if too narrow a definition of 'training' is adopted . If then is added the standard 'punitive' response to non-compliance, with penalties which may be unenforceable and may 'criminalise' young people and their families, the result will be further disaffection and an enduring dislike of anything to do with education. Indeed, if students are able to achieve suitable qualifications earlier, there may be very good reasons not to require it. Many students on work experience

---

[144] Harlen, W. & Deakin Crick, R. (2002). A systematic review of the impact of summative assessment and tests on students' motivation for learning. London: EPPI-Centre, Social Science Research Unit, Institute of Education.

are impressing employers with their skills and their maturity and such success must be carefully nurtured. In the same way, promoting higher education as the optimum pathway does not enhance the self-esteem or well-being of those who do not continue with education or of those who do and then drop out. Personalised learning should increase the flexibility relating to different kinds of learning and training at different ages.

Staff in schools know how important it is to build up relationships of trust and respect. Such relationships are not developed only in classrooms, but through form tutoring, participation in enrichment activities and incidental conversations in the dining room, on the sidelines during a football match, in a personal crisis. Good teachers are remembered with affection and respect, not only for their expertise in teaching and learning, but for their humanity and the values which they promote. Vulnerable students, many of whom suffer from unstable relationships at home, or find themselves far from respected by family or peers, benefit from a different perspective school staff can provide. In these second homes, parenting has to be distributed according to individual need and this may mean an investment of resources to address those with all kinds of special needs and to encourage independence. In schools in more challenging circumstances, support and encouragement are particularly vital, and there is a significant role for schools and those who work in them to provide stability and a consistent and affirming approach.

The capacity of school staff for such provision is in turn related to the extent to which their efforts are recognised and rewarded. For if students need praise and encouragement, so do schools. All human beings flourish with a proper recognition of what they are contributing. Those engaged in working with young people, especially with those who present particular challenges, need much encouragement. Inevitably, schools will have more or less vulnerable students. Some may in fact gain a reputation for their provision and care for them. These schools will almost certainly need to allocate more resources to engage them and meet their needs. Many at Key Stage 4 benefit from more vocational practical courses and these are often expensive, but they help to motivate, raise self-esteem and provide opportunities for success. Much time and effort is spent on establishing timetables to suit individual needs and in providing the necessary day-to-day support. Such efforts deserve proper acknowledgement.

All students and particularly vulnerable young people, benefit from stability. All schools therefore need to operate in a stable climate. They cannot afford to be diverted from their objectives by constant changes and by superficial judgments based on limited and flawed criteria which threaten their very existence. Vulnerable students need calm, supportive and enthusiastic adults, confident in their abilities to make a difference to the lives of young people. There are of course teachers who could teach better, subject departments which could provide more variety or challenge, schools which could be better managed or led. However, like the young people they serve, they cannot be written off. Teachers and leaders can develop skills and are encouraged to do so - that is the function of continuing professional development. Moreover, if the most able are to be recruited and, crucially, retained, the status of the profession and its mental health need the same nurture it provides for its students.

Schools must not be destroyed because an examination result appears to be poor.[145] Many schools currently in Special Measures can and will improve. They may need assistance with teaching and learning, with leadership, with support for their young people. In many ways, in relation to the five ECM outcomes, they may already be good schools. Individual families are not 'closed down'- however 'inadequate' they may be - unless there are health and safety issues. They are supported, encouraged and offered

---

[145]'Brown threat to close one in five schools unless results improve'. The Daily Telegraph 1st November 2007

110

strategies in ways which do not seek to undermine the authority of parents with their children. This contrasts starkly with some of the comments in inspectors' letters to children or in press releases from politicians which question teachers' abilities to improve and develop, undermine their authority and destroy their standing in the community. While theory demands that each individual should be valued and nurtured as a unique person, and personalised learning is promoted, practice often requires conformity. Those students who cannot or will not conform are too often isolated and rejected. Schools recognise this as a pattern which can result in the individual being the subject of bullying. The state must be careful that it does not itself engage in systematic bullying of schools and their collective rejection. Young people respond positively to encouragement, praise and recognition. So do schools.

Both government and local authorities have become poor corporate role models, advocating for students an inclusive and extended school, while increasingly constraining and narrowing their focus. Excessive health and safety constraints and punitive measures for failure to reach certain academic targets deter staff from organising exciting and life-changing experiences and foster anxiety and exclusion. Enterprise, innovation, creativity in curriculum development are heralded, while at the same time, the tests and examinations demand excessive curriculum time and drive effort. Pressure is justified by the need for accountability, paperwork abounds, and fear of failure and threats of consequences affect the work of both teachers and students.

If Every Child Matters is to be more than a slogan, schools need to have greater opportunities, facilities and recognition for the work they are doing with children who do not believe that they matter to anyone. Schools are in fact engaged in parenting. They will all be different – they will have strengths and weaknesses. They will be particularly good in some respects; they may develop certain specific interests and they will play to their strengths. Fundamentally however they are second homes, providing nurture, stability and positive influence. For many children schools are extensions of their family base – they provide the place where friends are met, interests are born and sustained, abilities are challenged, talents are developed and confidences shared. Teachers and other staff are indeed 'in loco parentis'.

Empowerment

Schools lie at the heart of their communities – whether as a village primary school or a city secondary school. They offer all young people amazing opportunities to discover themselves and other people, to understand what life in a society can be like, to experience, first and second hand, differences between people and to discover the excitement of learning. They provide havens of consistency, nurture and encouragement; they challenge and excite and set firm boundaries. They support parents in affirming the uniqueness of their child and the potential for him or her to be actively and positively involved in the society in which they live.

Schools are also rich community resources. Supporting young people means supporting their families and, when no one else will listen, someone at the school probably will. Enabling young people to grow and develop can mean many things to different people. Staff in schools speed up family housing matters, speak to shop managers about shoplifting incidents, provide references for Saturday jobs, attend funerals and comfort the bereaved, write court reports, advise families in debt or couples in difficulty to seek advice, courses or counselling or to visit the Citizen Advice Bureau. People do not forget kindness, and goodwill has an impact on the young person and on the attitudes of parents to their children's education. The coming together of Education, Health and Social Services under the Children Act and the establishment of locality teams to provide better communication between agencies and the 'team around the child' must be welcomed as an excellent development in safeguarding the future well-being of children. Together with the Extended Schools and Building

Schools for the Future initiatives the next decade could be an exciting and successful period for young people. However, without a greater recognition for the work being done in these areas and funding correspondingly increased, schools doing good work to enable young people to grow will be undervalued, demoralized and hamstrung.

The uniqueness of every student and the range of their life experience should make for caution in drafting policies which require all students to do the same things and to do them at or by a certain age. It is clear that young people are growing up fast in society. Primary school aged children can be found from an early age on the streets in the evenings mixing with older children. Their conversation includes sex, boyfriends, drinking and sometimes drugs and crime. They are targeted by advertisers to wear the latest fashions, look older than they are, buy and use sophisticated technology.[146] There is a need to reconsider what can be expected of them. While many commentators express anxiety about the decrease in childhood years, there is no doubt that society makes different demands on its young people and that the clock cannot simply be switched off or turned back. As young people mature in some ways more quickly, and skills increase, there may be underestimation of what they are capable of or can achieve at any given age. At the same time, however, some skills, for example literacy, may not be developing as expected and there may be less encouragement for young people to entertain themselves in a safe environment and to learn and study independently. It is also likely that demands for young people to behave as adults for good or bad outstrip their capacity for emotional maturity and their judgment may not be sufficiently developed to cope.

Maladjustment is not a word often used in research now – disaffection is more common. However, a maladjusted child, was, almost by definition, a child whose parent had uttered words of

---

[146] Daily Telegraph 10th December 2007

rejection – 'I don't want you, I will put you into care' (Stott 1982). Similar approaches to schools, it may be argued, produce collective maladjustment in a community. Where schools are labelled 'good', mobile parents will move closer, houses sustain their value and those who live around the school are pleased to be there. Where schools are labelled 'failing', some parents move away, the poverty of the community is underlined and a sense of community alienation and rejection heightened.

Each and every school can play a central part in their local community and the development of their young people. Schools need to have the confidence of the community and the whole-hearted support of local authorities, politicians, businesses and parents. There is much to celebrate and much progress being made by young people which cannot be measured by SATs or GCSE results. There is also much boredom, unhappiness and disaffection amongst a significant minority which can only end in tragedy for every community. At present, schools do not have sufficient freedom or funding to address the needs of these young people and fear of closure, censure and micro-management freezes enterprise, locks down creativity and causes anxiety in both staff and students. Once schools have the mandate to be adventurous, the time to devote to vulnerable individuals, the funding to address educational needs and the positive press to recognise and celebrate their success, much will be accomplished.

Education is not simply a preparation for the world of work. (Coffield, 2006) It is to enable young people to prepare themselves for life in a society. It assists, of course, in providing skills a workforce requires, including communication and personal skills, and in promoting the confidence which can lead to initiative taking, problem solving, flexible working and leadership skills. It is also preparing an individual for parenthood and for citizenship. Above all, education encourages self-analysis to recognise strengths and weaknesses, talents and skills and the personal growth of thinking and reflecting adults in a complex world. Being well-educated in a global sense means being aware of the cultures and beliefs, needs and strengths of others, respecting and valuing difference, being able to develop personal responses to events and experiences and acquiring a life-long capacity for learning. In other words, education is preparing an individual for a life which can be happy and fulfilled.

The most significant information for a secondary school which may be gained from a standardised test is the reading age of the students it is receiving, and their progress in reading thereafter. Other important information arrives from teacher assessment and conversations with staff in primary schools. If young people are to be empowered for life in a community, communication skills are vital and reading the corner stone of development and stability.

If every secondary school is to be empowered to become the centre of education for their communities, league tables as they exist at present must cease. With the arrival of 14-19 education partnerships, the introduction of diplomas and teaching shared across institutions, results could be declared publicly across partnerships or as county figures. Schools will then be able to take a full part in sustaining and raising achievement without being threatened, victimized or publicly shamed. Equally, support for disadvantaged students across the partnership is already beginning to lead to a heightened sense of community responsibility and will continue to do so. All schools will be seen as contributing to the achievement of all young people and each community school will be valued as the local member of a successful partnership.

If compulsory education and training is to be extended to 18, and if there is a real commitment to personalized learning, national statistics should be made public at 18+ when students have had opportunities to make progress at their own pace. A caring society should want to know the percentage of students at 18+ who have reading ages of 15+ (i.e. an adult reading age), or have achieved the equivalent of 5A*-G grades. Inclusion demands that all students know they have made progress and that they have engaged in a learning process which has enabled them to move into adult life, more confident of their ability to establish relationships and contribute to the happiness of themselves and others.

Some of the data which is now held in schools is helpful and can assist in planning and in assessing progress. All parents have a right to know that their children are making progress academically and it is motivating if progress made is at times accredited and success celebrated. But all parents equally have a right to know that their children are thriving, are happy and are learning more about themselves and their abilities. Schools can and do perform a major role in reducing deficit and enhancing self-esteem. No educational policies or strategies should be allowed to underline deficit, create anxiety or increase vulnerability. There are signs that if current policies continue as at present, the number of vulnerable young people will increase and society will notice the effects within local communities and in national statistics. Much good work is done now to nurture and encourage and to raise expectations and self-confidence, but progress relies too heavily on the work of talented individuals, teachers and support workers making relationships with young people, and coping with them as they live their lives on the margins. It needs to be underpinned by policy and funding.

Current policy is not addressing the aims of the 1944 Education Act, nor of subsequent Education Acts. Nor does it safeguard the five outcomes of the Every Child Matters agenda. In fact, the interests of children and young people are not the focus of much of present policy. That schools are functioning at all in the present climate is due to the leadership of headteachers and many other staff in schools working to reinterpret policy and guidance in the light of the needs of the young people, ignoring recommendations which are not in the interests of the students or schools, and talking up their schools in the local community. They are harnessing the obvious goodwill of local businesses and publicising through the media a wide range of successful experiences for their students. They are empowering many of their young people to make a positive contribution to society and to gain an understanding of responsible citizenship. They continue to try to hide their anxieties from the students they teach and often find themselves defending the school publicly and privately in the light of the latest media attack. Meanwhile, they expect and often witness high standards of achievement – and sometimes miracles. They encourage the values that society professes to believe in, watch students grow in self-esteem and respect for each other, and celebrate success. They empower many vulnerable students whom they are able to reach, to move to further and higher education, to enter local business with training prospects and most importantly to understand what it will take to be good parents and citizens. At the same time, they are only too aware of those they have been unable to reach and their poor future prospects.

It has never been more important for all those involved in education – staff, students, parents, governors, local communities - to decide on the purposes of compulsory education. Despite the contradictory messages and punitive policies, headteachers continue to make for themselves room to manoeuvre, in order to maintain the personal and corporate vision for their school in the local community. If the task of educators is to maximise the potential of each child as a human being living in society, then schools need freedom to tailor courses to individuals and to take into account local needs and opportunities without the same kind of anxiety, caused by the repeated criticism and the fear of rejection, which damages so many vulnerable students.

Twenty years ago, Lowe (1988), commenting on the new Education Reform Act of 1988, wrote:

> "If the legislation was truly meant to be done for pupils and not to them, once again it will be up to school staff and governors to ensure that it is so. The teaching profession has had plenty of practice at rescuing education from politics and despite all the

misgivings it will be so again, because the government needs teachers to deliver the 'reforms' and will know that teachers will only accept measures that can be demonstrated to be in the best interests of the children." (SHA 1988)

In closing the achievement gap, it is necessary to return to the aims of education in society, to award a higher profile to the needs of vulnerable students and to ensure that no policy is adding to their number. Young people can be born into disadvantage or develop disaffection or alienation through a complex series of events, family dysfunction, lifestyle and experience at home or at school. Society cannot afford to allow schools to contribute, through an imposed regime of targets, testing, league tables and inspection, to increasing the deficit or widening the achievement gap. Current policies caused by an inappropriate market model and micro-management for political ends are set to destroy the power of education to provide opportunities for happiness, achievement and success. In times when gloom and misery threaten to engulf many vulnerable individuals, teachers and support staff in schools sustain light in their communities. They are committed to professions which are privileged to make a difference to the lives of young people and which believe in the educational process of raising expectations, encouraging and praising individuals and celebrating their success. They need the freedom and resources to empower young people to take control of their own lives and enhance the lives of those around them.

RECOMMENDATIONS

Values

- The fundamental aims of education in society must be reflected in education policy and practice.

- Government agencies and local government need to model good 'parent' behaviour – encouraging and supporting, setting boundaries, adopting a 'can do' philosophy, providing additional support where need is the greatest. The market model is inappropriate and damaging.

- The government needs to recognise that the quality of education cannot be judged by examination results alone. There needs to be public recognition that schools are serving students and the communities in which they exist in many different ways.

- It is imperative that all those involved in education stop talking about closure, sacking and failure and start listening to young people and parents who are keen to support their local school and to develop its potential to serve the community.

- The language used in the development and support of schools requires urgent attention. It must be more positive and affirming.

Expectations

- Removing the KS2 and KS3 tests would result in wholly positive gain, especially for students with learning needs and those who, for any reason, are vulnerable. The considerable funding released should be given directly to schools to make greater provision for vulnerable young people.

- Schools need to keep records of reading ability on standardised tests. Such tests do not have to be reinvented each year, are criterion-referenced and are easily marked. More importantly, all students who struggle with reading would see progress from year to year based on their previous results. These would be more relevant than SATs, would assist self-evaluation and inspection, but should not be the subject of league tables.

- GCSE achievement at all grades A*-G must be recognised. Politicians and the media in particular need to stop talking about 'passing' and 'failing' within these grades. U is the only fail grade. Different grades will access different levels of further education; A*-G grades award at different levels and all can be passports to the future.

- The Government needs to understand the full implications of the current league table measure. Schools are now being judged on how many of their Year 11 cohort understand algebra to a C grade level or how many may have English as a second language. This is not an improvement on the previous 5 A*-C measure and places even more schools in danger of being talked down.

- There must be clarity about basic skills, particularly numeracy. If most adults do not use algebra, what skill is it that young people need to acquire? If such skills are accredited by Arithmetic GCSE or a Functional Skills test, then these and not GCSE Maths should be the baseline.

Encouragement

- If tests are intended to recognise ability and achievement, and reward levels of knowledge and understanding, they need to be taken when individual students are ready.

- As students mature more quickly, and learning is personalised, greater opportunities for fast-tracking of qualifications must be provided, especially for vulnerable students and those who are looked after. In some skills, ICT for example, or in Modern Languages, GCSE at the end of Year 9 may be more appropriate.

- Early identification of those for whom special education would be more appropriate would prevent tragedies in which young people transfer to mainstream schools where needs cannot be met. Appropriate provision must be found.

- The role of the many social, moral, spiritual and cultural opportunities schools provide for students needs to be more widely recognised as a key part of raising achievement for all. Such activities provide building blocks for experience of success.

- It is important that more expert assistance is available for students with mental health problems. Such assistance needs to be more immediate, with the potential for longer periods of support.

Empowerment

- All schools should receive Specialist Schools funding. Schools with higher percentages of vulnerable students stand to benefit the most from additional funding. The Specialised Schools Trust provides much support of quality which should be available to all.

- Results 14-19 should be declared across partnerships, preferably at 18+. This would empower personalized learning and promote inclusion.

- The funding of schools and other grants cannot be made available on the basis of the academic results of the schools. There is much evidence to indicate that it is the schools with the greater proportion of vulnerable students who need the most funding. The removal of KS2 and KS3 tests and the scaling down of Inspection would assist in provision for enrichment, extended schools, additional staffing and resources, to be determined by local need.

- Greater priority needs to be given to the recruitment and retention of good teachers. They need to be reassured that the profession is exciting, attractive, well-respected and rewarding, irrespective of their choice of school. The profession requires a higher status. There should be more opportunities for teachers to train as experts in Special Educational Needs.

- There needs to be sufficient special provision to meet students' needs. Special schools must be supported wholeheartedly as part of a policy of inclusion. They also provide 'second homes' for vulnerable young people. Their smaller scale provision suits some students and encourages them to make progress and the expertise of their staff is an under-used community resource.

- Many schools have established to good effect some small scale 'unit' provision - often speedily converted and seldom purpose built. Building Schools for the Future provides an opportunity to see whether more appropriate and better resourced small scale 'second homes' for vulnerable young people can be created within a mainstream school. Here students may access small group provision and the extra

122

nurture they may require, while at the same time being members of the wider school community.

- With self-evaluation, there should be less frequent whole-school inspections – once every six years would be sufficient. They should not be driven by academic statistics alone but should judge a school's contribution to the five ECM outcomes in a more balanced way. They should continue to pay particular attention to provision for and progress of vulnerable young people.

- Schools which are currently in Special Measures or labelled 'schools of concern' need additional support. Their contribution to the local community needs to be recognised and praised in order that confidence is restored.

BIBLIOGRAPHY

Alexander, Robin. (2004) Still no pedagogy? Principle, pragmatism and compliance. *Cambridge Journal of Education* 34 (1) pp 26-31

Audit Commission (1996) Misspent Youth: Young People and Crime

Barton Geoff (2007) Shouldn't Ofsted be helping us to improve our schools? *National Education Trust*

Bell, D. (2003) Access and achievement in urban education: 10 years on. *A speech to the Fabian Society, London 20th November 2003 in guardian.co.uk*

Bell, John F. (2001) Patterns of subject uptake and examination entry 1984-1997. *Educational Studies.* 27 (2) 1 pp201-219 (19)

Black, Paul (1998) Learning, League tables and National Assessment: opportunity lost or hope deferred. *Oxford Review of Education* March 1998 24 (1) P 57-68 ISSN 0305-4985

Blair, T. (1996) Speech at Ruskin College, December 1996 Oxford

Boyle, B., Bragg J. & Papasolomontos C. (2006) Playing their game: is there equity in assessment? A longitudinal study into the relationship between disadvantage and secondary school performance standards. *European Conference on Educational Research* University of Geneva 13-15 Sept 2006

Brehony, K. (2005) Primary schooling under New Labour: The irresolvable contradiction of excellence and enjoyment *Oxford Review of Education*, 31:(1),pp 29-46

Casey, L., Davies, P., Kalambouka, A., Nelson., & Boyle B. (2006) The influence of schooling on the aspirations of young people with special educational needs. *British Educational Research Journal* 32 (2) pp 273-290

Child A. (2003) Why students lose interest in school and what we can do about it *Journal of In Service Education* 29 (2) June 2003 pp 325-352

Clarke, B. (1997) Affirming the Comprehensive Ideal Ed. R Pring and G Walford London, Palmer

Coe, R. (2000) Target setting and feedback: can they raise standards in schools? Durham, University of Durham Curriculum Evaluation and Management Centre

Coffield, F. (2006) Running Ever Faster Down the Wrong Road: An Alternative Future for Education and Skills Inaugural Lecture

Connolly, P. (2006) The effects of social class and ethnicity on gender differences in GCSE attainment: a secondary analysis of the Youth Cohort Study of England Wales 1997-2001 *British Educational Research Journal,* 32 (1) April 2006 pp3-21

Cooper, P, Smith C., & Upton G (1993) Emotional and Behavioural Difficulties. London, Routledge

Croxford, L. (1999) League tables: who needs them? *CES Briefing* No 14 Centre for Educational Sociology

Davies, J. D., & Lee J. (2006) To attend or not to attend? Why some students chose school and others reject it. *Support for Learning*, 21 (4) pp 204-209

Davies, P., Coates G., Hammersley-Fletcher, L. & Mangan, J. (2005) When becoming a 50% school is success enough: a principal-agent analysis of subject leaders' target setting. *School Leadership and Management* 25 (5) 493-511

Department for Education Pupils with Problems (circulars 8-13) 1992

Durrant D. (2007) The role of UK Local Authorities to support school improvement Paper presented at the British Educational Research Association Annual Conference,

Earl L.M., Fullan, M., Leithwood, K. & Watson, N. (2000) Watching and Learning 3: OISE/UT evaluation of the Implementation of the Literacy and Numeracy Strategies Nottingham, DfEE Publications

Edmonds, S, Sharp, C Benefield, P (2002) Recruitment and Retention on Initial Teacher training: a Systematic Review Slough NFER

Evans C. A. & Docking J. (1996) Improving the Quality of Supportive Measures for Children with Learning Difficulties. *Early Child Development and Care* 121 (1) pp107-118

Every Child Matters (2003) Green Paper Published by The Stationery Office

Furlong V.J. (1991) Disaffected Pupils: Reconstructing the Sociological Perspective, *British Journal of Sociology of Education,* 12 (3) pp. 293-307.

Gorard S. (2005) Value-added is of little value. Paper presented at British Educational Research Association Annual Conference Glamorgan

Gray J. (2000) Causing concern but improving: – a review of schools' experiences. *Research Report No 188 Univ. of London*

Harlen W, Deakin Crick R (2002) A systematic review of the impact of summative assessment and tests on students' motivation for learning. In: *Research Evidence in Education Library*. London: EPPI-Centre, Social Science Research Unit, Institute of Education, University of London

Headmasters and Headmistresses Conference (HMC) (2004) School League Tables What they tell you…and what they don't. *Advice to Parents and Other Interested Parties Information paper*

Hilton, Z. (2006) Disaffection and School exclusion: why are inclusion policies still not working in Scotland. *Research Papers in Education* 21 (3) pp295-314

Howson John (2007) 13th Annual Survey of the Labour Market, NAHT/ASCL

Humphrey, N., Newton, I., & Charlton, J.P.(2004) The developmental roots of disaffection. *Educational Psychology* 24 (5) 2004 pp579-594

Jesson D. (2007) The use and misuse of CVA. *British Educational Research Association in Research Intelligence* 100 Article 5 p 23

Keele University, Centre for Successful Schools (2004) Schools Survey year averages

Keys W. (2006) Student Choices and Values in England, *European Journal of Education* 41(1) pp85-96

Kinder K. (1997) Talking back: Pupils' Views on Disaffection. National Foundation for Educational Research Slough

Kratzig, G. P. & Arbuthnott, K.D. (2006) Perceptual Learning Style and Learning Proficiency: A Test of the Hypothesis. *Journal of Educational Psychology* 98 (1) 238-246

Levacic, R. & Woods, P. (2002) A Raising School Performance in the League Tables (Part 1) disentangling the effects of social disadvantage. *British Education Research Journal* 28 (2)

Lindsay, G,. & Muijs D., (2006) Challenging underachievement in boys. *Educational Research* 48 (3) pp 313-332

Lovey, J. (2000) Disengagement, Truancy and Exclusion, New Labour's Policies for Schools ed J Docking David Fulton London Ch.12 page 201

Lovey, J., Docking, J. & Evans, R. (1993) Exclusion from School: provision for disaffection at KS4, David Fulton

Lowe, C. (1988) Education Reform Act 1988 Implications for School Management Secondary Heads Association.

Mansell, W. (2007) Education by Numbers: The Tyranny of Testing. Politico's.

McKinsey Report (2007) How the world's best performing school systems come out on top.

Merrett G. (2006) Higher standards, better schools for all - a critique; can market forces close the social and achievement gap? *Improving schools;* 9; 93 Sage publications

Miliband, D. MP (2004) Choice and Voice in Personalised Learning, Speech at a DfES Innovation Unit/Demos/OECD Conference 'Personalising Education: The Future of Public Sector Reform

Mitchell, G. & Hirom, K. (2002) The role of explanatory style in the academic underperformance of boys. *European Conference on Educational Research,* Lisbon 11-14 2002

Ofsted (1998) Secondary Education 1993-1997 A review of secondary education schools in England, Office for Standards in Education

Ofsted (2006) The Annual Report of Her Majesty's Chief Inspector 2006-2007, The Office for Standards in Education, Childrens' Services and Skills.

Organisation of Economic Cooperation and Development (OECD) (2007) Education at a glance

Parsons, C. (1999) Education, Exclusion and Citizenship, Routledge

Parsons, C. (2005) School Exclusion: The will to punish, *British Journal of Educational Studies* 53(2) pp 187-211

Perryman, J. (2007) Inspection and Emotion *Cambridge Journal of Education* 37 (1) pp173-190

Ray, A. (2006) School Value Added Measures in England. A Paper for the OECD Project on the Development of Value-Added Models in Education Systems Department for Education and Skills

Ranson, S. (1997) For citizenship and the remaking of civil society, Affirming the Comprehensive Ideal Ed. R Pring and G Walford London, Palmer

Reay D., Wiliam D. (1999) 'I'll be a nothing': structure, agency and the construction of identity through assessment. *British Educational Research Journal* 25 (3) pp343-354

Reed, J. & Hallgarten, J. (2003) Time to say goodbye? The future of school performance tables www.leeds.ac.uk/educol/documents/00003500.htm P18

Reid, K (2006) An evaluation of the views of secondary staff towards school attendance issues *Oxford Review of Education* 32 (3) 303-324

Riley, K., & Docking, J. (2004) Voices of Disaffected pupils: Implications for Policy and Practice. *British Journal of Educational Studies* 52 (2) June 2004 pp166-179

Riley, K., & Rustique-Forrester E. (2002) Working with Disaffected students London, Paul Chapman

Riley, K A (1998) Whose School is it Anyway? London, Falmer Press

Robinson, C. & Taylor, C. (2007) Theorising student voice: values and perspectives. *Improving Schools* 2007; 10, 5

Robinson, P. (1999): "The Tyranny of League Tables: international comparisons of educational attainment and economic performance." In R. Alexander, P. Broadford, D. Phillips, eds, Learning from Comparing. *New Directions in Comparative Education Research.* Volume 1 pp. 217 - 235. Oxford.

Rudduck, J. & Flutter, J. (2000) Pupil participation and pupil perspective: 'craving a new order of experience', *Cambridge Journal of Education* 30 (1) pp 75-89 Page 82

Sandford, R. A., Armour, K. M. & Warmington, P. C. (2006) Re-engaging disaffected youths through physical activity programmes. *British Educational Research Journal* 32 (2) April 2006 pp251-271

Scanlon, M. (1999) The impact of Ofsted Inspections NFER 0700515542

Searle Chris (2001) *An Exclusive Education. Race, class and exclusion in British schools* Lawrence and Wishart

Smithers, A. & Robinson, P. (2003) Factors affecting Teachers Decision to leave the Profession Nottingham, DfES

Solomon, Y. & Rogers C. (2001) Motivational Patterns in Disaffected School Student: insights from pupil referral unit clients. *British Educational Research Journal* (2001) 27 (3) 331-346

Stott, Denis (1982) Helping the Maladjusted Child. The Open University Press

Thomas S., Peng W. J., and Gray, J. (2007) Value added trends in English secondary education school performance across ten cohorts. *Oxford Review of Education* 33(3) 261-295

Thrupp, M. (1999) Schools Making a Difference: Let's Be Realistic. Buckingham Open University Press

Thrupp, M. & Tomlinson, S. (2005) Introduction: education policy, social justice and 'complex hope'. *British Educational Research Journal* 31 pp549-556

Torgenson, C. (2001) The evidence of misleading statistics in local education authority League Tables. *Curriculum* 22 (1) p 26-29 ISSN 0143-8689

Tymms, P. (2004) Are standards rising in English primary schools? *British Educational Research Journal* 30 (4) pp 477-494

UNICEF (2007) An overview of child well-being in rich countries. Report Card 7

Vulliamy, G. & Webb, R. (2003) Supporting disaffected pupils: perspectives from the pupils, their parents and their teachers. *Educational Research* 45 (3) 275-286

Whitty G., Power, S., Halpin D. (1998) Devolution and Choice in Education: The School, the State and the Market, Open University Press

Wiggins, A. & Tymms, P. (2000) Dysfunctional effects of Public Performance Indicator systems: a comparison between English and Scottish Primary schools. *European Conference on Educational Research* Edinburgh 20-23 Sep.

Woods, P. A. & Levacic, R. (2002) Raising School Performance in the League Tables Part 2 barriers to responsiveness in three disadvantaged schools. *British Educational Research Journal*, 28 (2) pp 227-247

Wright, C., Weekes, D., McGlaughlin, A. (2000) Race, Class and Gender in Exclusion from School, Studies in Inclusive Education. Falmer Press

Oxfordshire Secondary Schools League Tables – Rank Order

	1993	1994	1995	1996	1997	1998	1999	2000	2001	2002	2003	2004	2005	2006	2007
1	6	1	1	1	5	10	7	12	1	4	5	5	10	12	10
2	30	14	18	27	20	16	20	18	20	23	21	21	18	20	17
3	12	19	23	13	27	20	18	17	21	19	30	29	16	21	25
4	2	6	7	7	6	2	1	8	3	9	6	7	12	2	8
5	23	25	21	16	29	22	29	22	29	28	27	26	29	27	27
6	3	11	8	20	7	8	5	1	3	8	10	10	8	13	4
7	29	22	25	23	22	29	26	32	30	31	26	25	27	29	30
8	9	28	33	22	11	14	17	19	11	16	22	20	23	18	26
9	21	18	11	21	17	27	19	13	26	24	18	18	20	26	7
10	35	34	30	29	32	33	32	34	34	33	31	31	31	32	31
11	17	8	14	9	16	19	9	16	13	13	20	19	22	15	14
12	11	16	4	6	4	6	14	11	8	18	16	16	19	23	5
13	25	23	24	28	19	17	23	27	28	32	33	30	20	22	20
14	4	10	9	10	10	4	4	3	2	7	8	8	7	10	13
15	19	21	17	11	21	21	16	7	13	3	3	2	2	5	11
16	5	3	3	12	3	3	3	4	8	1	1	1	5	3	1
17	14	32	32	25	23	28	28	25	23	20	28	22	17	17	16
18	16	7	15	18	12	11	15	2	19	5	2	3	13	14	12
19	14	15	6	3	14	5	8	9	7	9	11	11	11	16	22

	1993	1994	1995	1996	1997	1998	1999	2000	2001	2002	2003	2004	2005	2006	2007
20	24	29	28	25	28	23	30	24	30	27	29	28	28	30	**28**
21	1	12	11	2	18	12	11	13	24	17	19	17	25	24	**24**
22	32	33	34	33	30	34	34	31	33	34	34	32	32	34	**33**
23	8	8	10	14	15	15	13	23	16	21	15	15	15	19	**18**
24	33	35	35	35	35	35	35	35	35	35	35	33	33	33	**32**
25	28	26	26	31	24	30	25	28	25	29	28	27	24	31	**29**
26	7	4	5	8	2	7	10	5	5	6	4	4	1	9	**18**
27	18	13	19	15	9	13	20	15	11	15	12	13	9	6	**8**
28	10	2	2	5	1	1	2	6	5	2	7	6	4	1	**2**
29	13	5	13	4	12	9	5	10	15	14	14	14	5	7	**15**
30	27	24	20	30	32	18	22	26	21	25	25	24	14	28	**23**
31	22	20	16	17	8	24	24	20	8	12	9	9	3	4	**6**
32	26	17	22	18	16	26	11	21	17	11	12	12	8	11	**3**
33	31	27	27	32	30	32	31	30	26	26	24	23	26	25	**21**

Note:
2 schools are not included in the ranking because they closed during this period.
Originally 35 schools.
2007 (in bold type) the new measure —5A*-C with English and Maths

APPENDIX 2

From Inspection Reports – 2005-2006

The extent to which schools enable learners to be healthy	
Learners are encouraged and enabled to eat and drink healthily	Yes
Learners are encouraged and enabled to take regular exercise	Yes
Learners are discouraged from smoking and substance abuse	Yes
Learners are educated about sexual health	Yes
The extent to which providers ensure that learners stay safe	
Procedures for safeguarding learners meet current government requirements	Yes
Risk assessment procedures and related staff training are in place	Yes
Action is taken to reduce anti-social behaviour, such as bullying and racism	Yes
Learners are taught about key risks and how to deal with them	Yes
The extent to which learners make a positive contribution	
Learners are helped to develop stable, positive relationships	Yes
Learners, individually and collectively, participate in making decisions that affect them	Yes
Learners are encouraged to initiate, participate in and manage activities in school and the wider community	Yes
The extent to which schools enable learners to achieve economic well-being	
There is provision to promote learners' basic skills	Yes
Learners have opportunities to develop enterprise skills and work in teams	Yes
Careers education and guidance is provided to all learners in key stage 3 and 4 and the sixth form	Yes
Education for all learners aged 14-19 provides an understanding of employment and the economy	Yes

APPENDIX 3a
Secondary Headteachers' Questionnaire

November 2007

Note: In what follows- current policies = targets, league tables, inspections, government guidance etc.

1. Do you think that current policies have influenced you to increase/decrease the number of fixed term or permanent exclusions? – If so, how?

2. (a) In the last three years, has your school gained additional funding/ support to introduce strategies to raise standards? If so, from which source? e.g. Specialist Schools Trust?

2 (b) If so, for what group of students has the funding been targeted?
     e.g. L6+ English, 4/5 borderline, Boys A*-C, C/D borderline etc.

3. Has your school decided to initiate strategies (not externally funded) in relation to specific groups of students? If so, please give brief details.

4. Has the change in statistics from 5A*-C /5A*-G to 5A*-C / 5A*-G with E/M influenced the policies of the school ? e.g. re curriculum offer, introduction of new qualifications, entry policies

5. Have current policies changed your policies towards entering pupils for Entry Level qualifications or Level 1 vocational courses ? If so, how?

6. Has the 'capped 8' APS influenced decisions about GCSE entry or courses available? If so, which group(s) of students have been affected? Please give details

7. Do your whole school targets influence the work of your pupils or your teaching staff from year to year? Please explain.

8. Do staff perceive motivational issues in relation to individual target setting for students likely to achieve –say D-G grades, or Level 4 at KS3? If so, how does the school deal with this?

9. *Note: This question is not about <u>procedures</u> in place e.g. MQ(Monitoring Quality)1 and 2 but about influence.*
To what extent does the Local Authority influence you, your staff and your governors in
- a.   setting targets
- b.   identifying strategies to improve performance
- c.   decisions relating to exclusions?

10. Do you see evidence in your school of disaffection caused by a perception of academic failure. If so, please can you elaborate - evidence on entry in Yr 6? particular year groups? what kind of disaffection?

11. Could you identify –from last summer's results- students who through social disadvantage did not perform as well as FFT or internal prediction would have estimated? If so, what kinds of disadvantage were in evidence?

12. Any other comment on these topics you would like to make?
 e.g? Headteacher views on the job now with the current pressures
Does the pressure teachers feel communicate itself to students – less prepared to put up with the disaffected?

Would you be prepared to allow me to follow up any of this information?
YES/NO
If so, please give your name..

Many thanks for your time

Cynthia Bartlett

APPENDIX 3b

Supplementary questionnaire
Many thanks to all those who have replied to my first questionnaire.

The following questions are by way of follow-up arising from issues heads have raised
They are of the single word answer sort! Please underline or indicate in any way the answers

Does your school provide breakfast?

Open to all

| | Yes | No |

Provided for a group of vulnerable students

| | Yes | No |

Would it be fair to say that, in subjects set by ability, Subject Leaders take care to ensure that Year 9 borderline 4/5 and at KS4 C/D borderline sets have good teachers?

| | Yes | No |

The 5A*-G target is not now compulsory – are you still setting a target for 5A*-G?

| | Yes | No |

Since the workforce remodelling, have you appointed a non-teaching Student Welfare Manager or equivalent?

| | Yes | No |

Do you test students reading ages every year?

All Years

| | Yes | No |

Just Year 7

| | Yes | No |

Visits/Residentials/Visits Abroad etc.
Would you say that the level of offer of these to students compared to - say -7-
10 years ago is

                                          Greater than before
                                          About the same
                                          Less than before?

Many thanks

Cynthia Bartlett

Printed in Great Britain
by Amazon.co.uk, Ltd.,
Marston Gate.